# Political Parties, U.S.A.

RAND MᶜNALLY PUBLIC AFFAIRS SERIES

# Political

ESSAYS BY

STEPHEN K. BAILEY

EDWARD C. BANFIELD

WALTER BERNS

HARRY V. JAFFA

CHARLES M. HARDIN

MORTON GRODZINS

HERBERT J. STORING

# Parties, U.S.A.

EDITED BY

ROBERT A. GOLDWIN

RAND MᶜNALLY & COMPANY • CHICAGO

# PREFACE

●

Politically minded people the world over seem to hold an un-
flattering opinion of American political parties, an opinion
shared not only by the enemies of free government but by many
of its most devoted friends and dedicated spokesmen as well.
How can this be explained?

The criticisms of American parties are numerous. They do
not have clearly defined programs of political action which offer
the voters meaningful alternatives. The party in office cannot be
held responsible for legislation, because party members in Congress are free to vote as they wish in the almost complete absence
of party discipline. Party structure is such that the local parties
are more permanent than the national parties, with the result
that local issues tend to prevail over national issues, private and
sectional advantage over the general welfare. This dominance of
partial interests over the public good produces parties that cannot free themselves from patronage and the widely deplored
spoils system.

American parties are so unlike the political parties elsewhere
that one of the authors in this volume suggests that they are
really not parties at all; they are rather "antiparties," for they
prevent the formation in the United States of what are elsewhere considered true parties.

The present authors take as their starting point the sense of
confusion and dissatisfaction shared by ordinary citizens, interested foreigners, party politicians, and students of the American
political process. Many of their conclusions are, to say the least,
surprising. In this volume are encountered the arguments that

## Preface

reforms now possible can make our parties more democratic and responsive to the will of their members; on the contrary, that without those features most commonly condemned as undemocratic, we would lose the most democratic political results; that the results most deplored can be remedied without resort to reform of the parties; on the contrary, that only drastic constitutional revision can correct the defects of our party system; that our two-party system is fundamentally a one-party system and that if it were not it could not continue as an effective two-party system; and, finally, that a major task of party leaders should be to co-operate in giving the civil service a character more political —in a certain sense of that word—than it presently has.

These essays, taken together, are a varied, profound, and comprehensive inquiry into the true nature of our political system.

R. A. G.

March, 1964

# CONTENTS

•

# THE EDITOR AND THE AUTHORS

•

ROBERT A. GOLDWIN

is Lecturer in Political Science and Director, Public Affairs Conference Center, The University of Chicago. He is the editor of *Readings in World Politics*, 5th ed., 1959; *Readings in American Foreign Policy*, 4th ed., 1959; and *Readings in Russian Foreign Policy*, 3rd ed., 1959.

STEPHEN K. BAILEY

is Professor of Political Science, Maxwell Graduate School of Citizenship and Public Affairs, Syracuse University. His political activity has included service as Administrative Assistant to Senator William Benton; as Mayor of Middletown, Connecticut; and as Consultant to the Research Division of the Democratic National Committee. His books include *Roosevelt and His New Deal*, 1933; *Congress Makes a Law*, 1950; *Congress at Work*, 1951; and *Government in America*, 1957.

EDWARD C. BANFIELD

is Professor of Government, Harvard University, and a staff member of the Joint Center for Urban Studies of the Massachusetts Institute of Technology and Harvard University. His fields of study include urban politics and city planning. He is the author of *Government Project*, 1951; *Politics, Planning and the Public Interest*, 1955 (with Martin Meyerson); *Government and Housing in Metropolitan Areas*,

# The Editor and the Authors

1958 (with Morton Grodzins); *The Moral Basis of a Backward Society*, 1958; *Political Influence*, 1960; and *City Politics*, 1963 (with James Q. Wilson).

WALTER BERNS

Professor of Government, Cornell University, specializes in the field of constitutional law. He is the author of *Freedom, Virtue and the First Amendment*, 1957, and articles in various political science and legal periodicals.

HARRY V. JAFFA

is Professor of Political Science, The Ohio State University. His fields of specialization are political philosophy and American political thought. He is the author of *Thomism and Aristotelianism*, 1952; and *Crisis of the House Divided*, 1959; and editor of *In the Name of the People*, 1960 (with R. W. Johannsen).

CHARLES M. HARDIN

Associate Director, Humanities and Social Science, The Rockefeller Foundation, is a former Professor of Political Science, The University of Chicago. His special fields of study are agricultural politics and political parties. He is the author of *The Politics of Agriculture*, 1952, and *Freedom in Agricultural Education*, 1955.

MORTON GRODZINS

late Professor of Political Science, The University of Chicago, was the author of *Americans Betrayed*, 1949; *The Loyal and the Disloyal*, 1956; and *Government and Housing in Metropolitan Areas*, 1958 (with Edward C. Banfield). His special field of study was American political parties.

HERBERT J. STORING

is Associate Professor of Political Science, The University of Chicago, specializing in the study of public administration and constitutional law. He is author of *The State and the Farmer*, 1962 (with Peter Self), and editor and joint author of *Essays on the Scientific Study of Politics*, 1962.

STEPHEN K. BAILEY

•

# OUR NATIONAL POLITICAL PARTIES*

This essay attempts to defend three propositions:

*One:* Our system of national political parties is intimately related to the difficulties, dangers, and opportunities that now face the United States as a political community and a world power.

*Two:* A series of reasonably modest changes in the national party system would greatly strengthen America's capacity to govern responsibly and effectively.

*Three:* These changes are now possible as a result of great secular shifts in our social and economic life which are undermining traditional citadels of political power.

If I did not believe in the truth of the third proposition, this paper would not have been written. But evidence leads me to believe that the old party system is disintegrating. Whether something better will take its place depends, first, upon the capacity of creative minds to suggest revisions suited to a new political era; second, upon the capacity of political leadership to build consent for translating the proposals into reality.

## THE PARTIES AND RESPONSIBLE POWER

The American government today suffers from three weaknesses:

1. its difficulty in generating sustained political power;

2. its difficulty in developing a flow of imaginative, informed, consistent, and power-related responses to pressing national and world issues;

*This essay is abridged and adapted by the author from his paper, "The Condition of Our National Political Parties," published by The Fund for the Republic, 1959.

1

3. its difficulty in making policy truly accountable to a national popular majority.

These are serious defects, not only because they interfere with wise and coherent governing in these dangerous days, but because they undermine the faith of the citizen in the reality or even the possibility of responsible representative government.

The defects are not new. Occasionally, in the past, they have been masked by brilliant presidential leadership in times of crisis or by the virtuosity of congressional leaders in times of presidential ineptitude. But the underlying defects have not disappeared. It is increasingly obvious that there are innovative, integrative, and perhaps sacrificial tasks ahead for which our government is not institutionally equipped.

At first glance, the problem seems to be constitutional—and in part it is. But the real problem is *political*. If our *political* institutions can be modernized by certain changes in statutory law and in political party rules, the old problems associated with separation of powers, checks and balances, and federalism would, it seems probable, largely disappear.

The root of the weakness is that while the two national parties for years have genuinely competed for the Presidency they have not made a similar effort in the election of United States Senators and Members of the House of Representatives. Nor have they been of sufficient help to the President and the Congress in providing candidates of high quality for the grand patronage of departmental and agency direction. So long as we lack strong national parties operating as catalysts in the Congress, the executive branch, and the national government and state and local governments, power will continue to be dangerously diffused or, perhaps what is worse, will whipsaw between diffusion and presidential dictatorship.

Political reform does not include making the parties any more ideological than they are now. It does include making them competitive across the nation, allowing them to appeal to the natural ideological divisions within the population and within us as individuals. The stumbling block in this task is that neither party has a sufficiently unified structure to enable it to dramatize its program around its ideology; neither has the power, even if it had the right structure, to carry out the program; neither has sufficiently clear and unambiguous lines of political accountability running to the voters.

The structural limitations of the parties have grave consequences. First, they virtually insure a government by fits and starts. For example, presidential requests for an adequate United States Information Agency budget have been listened to one year and ignored the next by the House Appropriations Committee. As a result, cultural officers abroad have had to spend much of their time hiring and firing—inflating and deflating programs like an accordion. This has made us look ridiculous as a nation, and has also made it extremely difficult for a coherent information program to develop as a vital element in our foreign policy. The same has been true of foreign economic aid.

Spasms in domestic policy have been equally obvious and equally unsettling. The executive department and the Congress have been unable to agree on any coordinated methods of applying the kind of devices needed to stabilize the economy and promote the goals of the Employment Act of 1946. Similar fits and starts have been noticeable in defense policy, atomic energy policy, welfare policy, and conservation policy. They have been quite as apparent when the Presidency and both Houses of Congress have been in one party as when the control of the government has been divided.

The second consequence of the structural limitations of the parties has been the lack of rationality and consistency in the substance of much public policy. In a world in which, for example, the indiscriminate dumping of rice on the world market in order to ease a temporary glut in Louisiana could cost us the friendship of Burma, there are huge dangers in having unlinked centers of power making their own policy for the nation. And yet, parochial groups in the Congress (often in league with sections of the executive branch and with outside pressure groups) still carry an inordinate amount of power.

The third consequence of the absence of coherent party machinery truly responsive to popular majorities is that congressional compromise tends to fall with considerable regularity on the side of minority rather than majority interests. Committee chairmen from "safe," and often sparsely populated, one-party states and districts; the minority-weighted bipartisan rules committee; the myths, rules, and influence structure which enable congressional leaders to ignore demands for greater majority representation in policy decisions—all these combine to inflate the power of minority interests at the expense of the national popular majority.

This is government by tollgate. It leads directly to consequence four: the increasing danger of public cynicism and apathy toward the Congress, partly because its power is too diffuse or too subtle to comprehend; partly because when the power *is* clearly identifiable it seems to work more consistently for minorities than for the majority.

The last and by no means the least important consequence stemming from the absence of a unified party structure is that desperately needed criticism of both domestic and foreign policy is dissipated and discouraged. There is no effective vehicle for responsible criticism of programs by the opposition; there is no machinery for anticipating the implications of social changes and their effects on policy.

In sum, the absence of effective party machinery in each House, and in the government generally, means that policy is frequently developed by an infinitely intricate system of barter and legerdemain.

Some defenders of America's traditional disorder have discounted the dangers to policy-making of these intermittencies and irresponsibilities. They argue that our survival suggests that presidential leadership and a congressional desire to cooperate during periods of crisis can save us in the future as they have in the past; that the lulls between crises allow the divergencies in our society to have their day without being subject to the tyranny of a transient numerical majority; and that the accepted American tradition of government by extraordinary or "concurrent" majorities has not stopped innovation or social criticism: it has only slowed change, and in the process has insured a healthy unity behind public policy.

In relation to the past, these may be strong arguments. But are they addressed to a world of big bureaucracies, sustained cold wars, and chronic international and domestic crises? Are there any longer identifiable periods between crises? As long as the frontier was open and the spirit of laissez faire encouraged political parties to be barriers against government action, an-

4

archy in program and uncontrolled shifts in power within the national government were of little consequence.

But we are now in a very different world. Inexorable forces are now clearly at work preparing the soil for a crop of politics far different from what we have known in the past century. It is time for a stringent look at the national politics we have had, the kind of national politics we want, and the reasons for believing that our traditional party system, like a vast glacier, may now have reached the edge of the sea.

### The Parties Today: A Mystic Maze

The closer one gets to our two great national parties, the more difficult it is to find them. If one contends that they exist in their quadrennial national conventions, he must be prepared to answer where they are between conventions. If one identifies them with the national committee offices in Washington, or one of them with the White House, he will hear immediate disclaimers from the party leaders on Capitol Hill. If a temporary marriage should be negotiated between the party in Congress and the party's executive wing, the great cellular blocks of the party at the state and local levels might well ask embarrassing questions about the true locus of party power.

The long history of the parties shows that it would be a mistake to suggest that the national committees have been at the power apex of their parties. "Although the party organization can be regarded as . . . capped by the national committee, it may be more accurately described as a system of layers of organization. Each successive layer—county or city, state, national—has an independent concern about elections in its geographical jurisdiction. Yet each higher level of organization, to accomplish its ends, must obtain the collaboration of the lower layer or layers of organization. That collaboration comes about, to the extent that it does come about, through a sense of common cause rather than the exercise of command."[1]

The formal organization of the parties can be described, if at all, then, as a series of pyramids with a common base in the shifting sands of active party membership, and generally with no clear locus of power in or out of the government.

[1] V. O. Key, *Politics, Parties, and Pressure Groups* (4th ed.; New York: Crowell, 1958), p. 368.

5

This can best be highlighted by trying to answer a deceptively simple question: On matters of national policy, what individual or group speaks with authority for each of the national parties?

Let us start with a presidential election year and a national convention. The choice for the Presidency personifies the majority decision of the national convention, and in this respect the winning nominee speaks with special authority as a symbol of what the party stands for at that moment. From the moment of nomination until election, the presidential candidate is usually the undisputed voice of the party. This does not mean that the voice will necessarily be clear, but no other is likely to be clearer.

There is a circumstance, however, in which even this last generalization needs qualification. Special problems arise when an incumbent President and a new presidential nominee are of the same party. In 1952, for example, with Adlai Stevenson as the Democratic nominee but with Harry S. Truman still in the White House, a series of delicate issues developed over campaign strategy, organization, and policy. The National Committee found itself the center of a tug of war between the White House and Springfield. It was not until after the election that President Truman called Adlai Stevenson "the head of the nation's Democrats."

Apart from the kind of conventions and campaigns that may create unusual ambiguities of the sort just mentioned, the recognized spokesman for a national party controlling the Presidency (the in-party) is the President himself.

The extent to which a President can create the image of a reasonably united party, depends, of course, on his capacity to make his own policy pronouncements dominant in the party. This is not always automatic, especially if the President is successfully blocked by powerful leaders of his own party in the Congress or is running out the last two years of his last term. But, even then, the power of his voice generally reduces the voices of self- or group-appointed party spokesmen to a subordinate level.

If the in-party has problems in creating a clear party image, the task is many times more difficult for the out-party. No real answer has yet been found to the question of who speaks for the party when it does not control the White House, or when no presidential campaign is in progress. Over the years, some of the major contenders for the job of out-party spokesman have been congressional leaders, national committee chairmen, national committee executive committees, ex-Presidents, defeated presidential candidates, *ad hoc* groups established by the national committees, congressional policy committees, congressional campaign committees, and, most recently, a permanent advisory council to a national committee.

The contention that the leaders of the out-party in Congress have the responsibility and the right to speak for their party has been staunchly defended by those leaders. But, in the years since World War II, intramural struggles between national committee chairmen and spokesmen on the one hand, and congressional leaders and staff on the other, have been staples in out-party politics, regardless of which party was "out."

Obvious problems arise in having the congressional leaders speak for the out-party. Congress itself is bifurcated, and its power, as we have said, tends to gravitate into the hands of men who are not necessarily responsive to the party majorities. Even party leaders in the Congress, chosen in caucuses of their own party, are captives, willing or unwilling, of the feudal barons who immediately surround them. There are no party policy or steering committees in the House worthy of the name, and those in the Senate lack power and representativeness.

The absence of any fully accepted out-party national spokesman has led each party sporadically over the years to try to fill the vacuum.

Perhaps the most noteworthy out-party voice in recent years was the Democratic Advisory Council of the Democratic National Committee. Established by a resolution of the Executive Committee of the Democratic National Committee on November 27, 1956, the Council existed to provide "a collective voice for the Democratic Party, representing on a year-round basis the millions of Democrats who may or may not be represented in either House of the Congress." The official congressional leaders of the party refused membership on the Council, but many of the party's national figures belonged. The Council was helped in its deliberations by advisory committees of distinguished party intellectuals on such matters as foreign policy, domestic economic policy, labor policy, urban problems, science and technology, and party organization.

The Democratic Advisory Council was a significant development, to which we shall return. At the moment, it is sufficient to note that, although it gave the out-party a firmer voice and a clearer public philosophy than was available before, it had no effective power base in the party, it was not the only voice and image the out-party had, and the party portrait it painted was easily distorted or obscured by the record of the party in the Congress.

The problem of the out-party in developing a recognizable philosophy and coherent political program is further complicated by the disorganized state of its finances. Actually, the in-party is also haunted by the same specter. Money-raising for national and congressional campaigns is such a jungle, and so choked with the vines of subterfuge to get around the Hatch Act and other unrealistic laws, that efforts to develop coherent national party organizations are seriously impeded.

It is an axiom of congressional campaigning, for example, that little direct financial help can be expected either from Washington (campaign committees on Capitol Hill or the national committees) or from state committees. There are, of course, exceptions, but these are sufficiently rare to prove the rule.

Since the party as party (no matter how defined) has not been a sure source of financial help to the man campaigning for a seat in the Senate or House, what obligation does he owe to it, or to programs endorsed by it?

And there is a further complication. Some support for congressional candidates may come in the form of what Senator Benton used to call "emotional money"—money given by friends and admirers, with no strings attached. But much of it comes from constituent interests, or powerful national interests, expecting, if not favors, at least sympathetic understanding and ready access. It makes little difference if the President or an advisory council to a national committee comes out with a strong plea for more liberal foreign economic policies in the interests of national security and world economic development as long as powerfully placed Representatives or Senators are beholden financially to narrow anti-foreign aid and trade interests in their constituencies.

Attempts by the national committees to raise money for "the party" have gone largely into the staggering costs of presidential campaigns, past or present. And none of the four congressional campaign committees purports to take any interest whatsoever in a congressional candidate's policy stand or his identification with a party majority. They are interested in electing "Republicans" period, or "Democrats" period.

These, then, are our national parties: unified for presidential contests, otherwise divided in power and lacking in definition; sporadically financed through various channels, subterfuges, and individual candidacies; peculiarly confused as out-parties; weak vehicles for executive-legislative cooperation as in-parties. How should our national party system be modified in order to make the parties effective instruments of our national purposes and needs?

### NINE POLITICAL REFORMS

One reason why it is safe to suggest that the national party system must be strengthened in order to bring sustained power to our government is that the safeguards of the Constitution will continue to discourage any force that becomes so unified as to threaten our freedom. The American people hold firm to the sanctity of the Constitution. It is inconceivable that they would countenance a wholesale revision of the Constitution in the foreseeable future. No model of a new or improved party system that rests on substantial constitutional change is realistic.

In suggesting new directions for our national party system, therefore, the British parliamentary model is ruled out. But it is not ruled out simply because its wholesale adoption here is unthinkable. It is ruled out because it has shortcomings which do not warrant emulation. The relative independence of the legislature in the American system of government is, within limits, a powerful asset. At its best, it assures continuing social criticism and review of the bureaucracy without which big government might easily become lethargic and unresponsive or officious and dangerous.

What we are after is a national two-party system that will continue to have room for diversity and compromise but will

9

nevertheless bring about more coherent and responsible programming by the executive and legislative branches and more coherent and responsible criticism of policy and administration. We are after a system that will make parties compete vigorously to find the right answers; that will organize political power at the national level so that it is adequate to carry out those answers; and that will make this power ultimately accountable to popular majorities.

The following proposals neither presume nor suggest ideological or highly disciplined parties, although they do presume differences in the ideological propensities of each party and also presume that party members who vote consistently against their own party's majority will not be favored with positions of party power inside or outside the Congress.

#### 1. BROADLY-BASED FINANCING

If the national party were able to help finance even a small proportion of a Congressman's campaign, and thus reduce his dependency on local money, he might feel freer to weigh short-term local against long-term national interests or, more accurately, to weigh the special interests against the common interests within his own constituency.

To insure an increasingly responsible role for the national committees over national party finances, the Hatch Act provisions dealing with spending limitations for national campaigns should be repealed or realistically adjusted to meet the realities of political life. Furthermore, federal income-tax credits or exemptions should be allowed for individual contributions to the *national* organizations or candidates up to a certain amount.

The postage-franking privilege and a block of network television time, radio time, and newspaper advertising space should be given to each national committee before each national election, to be financed by congressional appropriations and rigidly audited by the General Accounting Office.

#### 2. TWO-PARTY COMPETITION

One of the most compelling reasons for the national committees to have more money is that greater riches may encourage more vigorous competition between the parties in all states and congressional districts in the country. Everything we know about one-party areas indicates that they tend to reflect minority interests and, through unopposed re-elections, produce Members of Congress who are pushed by seniority into positions of high and unrepresentative power.

"The variations in the degree to which the parties are competitive within their respective states condition in a major way the policy inclinations of Senators," V. O. Key writes. "Those from one-party states may be untouched by the great tides of national politics. On the other hand, Senators from close states may live under the strongest compulsion to collaborate among themselves in the promotion of the cause of their party nationally."[2]

The more quickly the national party organizations succeed in stimulating opposition in districts and states where there is none, or in narrowing the margin of the dominant party's victory, the better chance there is of relating the Congress more closely to the interests of the national majority.

The process can be speeded if the national committees are enabled to work with the congressional campaign committees on the Hill in supplementing the services of the state and local organizations to congressional campaigns and in providing regional representatives to help unify the several campaigns in a multi-state region like New England or the Middle West.

As the national committees become stronger financially and organizationally, their prestige will also grow to the point where they could have a much more positive influence on the choice of congressional nominees. Until that time, their interests, and those of the country, would seem to be best served by a thorough-going drive to strengthen two-party competition in all parts of the country. It is obvious that the most intractable one-party areas are in the South. The voting rights of Negroes and low-income whites should increase as a result of the Civil Rights Bill of 1957 and of the Supreme Court decision in 1962 in *Baker* v. *Carr*, enforcing greater equity in state legislative representation. But the solution to the most obvious indignities undergone by the disenfranchised is to speed the extension of two-party competition. This can be done not only by active organizing on the part of the Republican Party but by extending the influence of

[2] *Ibid.*, p. 593.

the national Democratic Party in registration and voting drives below the Mason-Dixon line.

### 3. ADVISORY COUNCILS

For the in-party, an advisory council is probably superfluous. But, at its best, an advisory council to an out-party's national committee can be a loyal opposition in the manner of the British shadow cabinet.

Although an advisory council should explicitly represent the executive wing of its party, it should include in its membership, at least as nonvoting observers, the congressional party leaders or their designates.

The two national conventions, as the ultimate governing bodies of the national parties, should formally sanction the establishment of advisory councils as permanent policy arms of the two national committees—latent in the case of the in-party, active in the case of the out-party.

### 4. PARTY CLUBS

The idea of having a "Democratic Club" and a "Republican Club" in Washington to house the national committees and congressional campaign staffs and to serve as a social head-quarters for the parties has been considered off and on for many years by both parties. Actually, *ad hoc* party clubs presently exist in Washington—but only for social purposes. If these clubs were given greater dignity and larger facilities for housing disparate party staffs, they would unquestionably promote more coordinated and efficient party efforts, not by hierarchy but by propinquity. Dues would help to finance general party activities. The clubs would stand as reminders that a sense of national community and forceful and responsible national action are functions of a competitive *two*-party system.

### 5. CONGRESSIONAL TERMS

The constitutional provisions for two-year terms for Congressmen and for staggered elections are a significant cause of the pullings and haulings in our national government and of congressional preoccupation with petty constituent errands.

A four-year term for the House—half the House being elected every two years—should have a number of important effects. Under normal conditions, it would promote the same political complexion for the House as the President's—at least half the time. It would reduce the continuous campaign and constituency pressures which a two-year term almost inevitably fosters. It would give Congressmen sufficient time to learn their trade and to make a substantial contribution to public life.

At the same time, the conservative utility of overlapping terms would be maintained with only a slight modification in the constitutional wish for continuity.

Enhancing the possibility of one-party control of the government would enhance the possibility of substantial governmental power and would help to fix responsibility for governmental policy. Political reality would probably dictate that incumbent Congressmen would have to be prohibited from running against an incumbent Senator of their own party in the middle of the congressional four-year term unless they resigned from the House. Otherwise, Senate support for a four-year term for Congressmen might be difficult to secure.

### 6. PARTY POLICY COMMITTEES IN THE CONGRESS

The Democrats in the Senate have placed their Majority Leader in charge of their policy committee. Lyndon Johnson's power came in large part from his own personal ability; but it seems certain that his leadership was strengthened by his policy committee role. The Majority Leader's power would more truly reflect the interests of the majority of his party in the Senate if the representative character of the policy committee were broadened and more caucuses were held. The Republican policy committee in the Senate is far more representative than its Democratic counterpart; what it needs is to be tied more closely to the operations of the Republican floor leader who is a member of the policy committee, but not its chairman.

With these changes, the example set by the Senate should be followed by the House of Representatives. Adequately staffed party policy committees should be elected in both Houses by caucus. In the House of Representatives, the Speaker should chair his party's committee; the Minority Leader should chair the minority party's committee. The majority policy committee should assume the functions of the House Rules Committee. Both policy committees should act as the committee on committees for their party, and should perform policy and steering functions presently scattered or moribund.

In order to bring greater cohesion to the handling of major presidential recommendations, the four policy committees should meet jointly for two weeks in late January and early February each year to conduct general hearings on the President's State of the Union message. The hearings should be widely covered by press, radio, and television; the leaders in the administration and in the out-party should be heard.

### 7. SENIORITY

The principle of seniority has always been defended in the Congress on the ground that it is the only system for elevation to positions of power that has the virtue of being automatic. Congress, it is argued, is already so charged with tension and conflict that additional struggles for power would be dangerous to the underlying agreement upon which compromise and unity rest.

There is enough weight to this argument to suggest that if responsible majority rule can be achieved without destroying the impersonal attributes of the seniority system, the system should be kept. However, there seems to be no reason why a simple mathematical formula cannot be devised to give added seniority credit to legislators who come from competitive two-party districts and states. For example, a Member might receive two points for every *general* election in which his opponent received more than 20 per cent of the vote. Seniority would still rule, automatically, but power would tend to shift toward those Congressmen who come from districts in which vigorous two-party competition searches out the majority interest.

### 8. THE TWENTY-SECOND AMENDMENT

The Twenty-Second Amendment places a two-term limit on American Presidents. Its effect is to weaken the political power and influence of the President in his second term, particularly in his last two years. At a time when foreign policy and national defense hold apocalyptic potentialities, it is madness to retain in our Constitution an Amendment which *guarantees* fitful national power.

### 9. EXECUTIVE TALENT

The strength and responsiveness of the national government depend upon many factors, but one of the most basic requirements is a core of able political executives to direct the sprawling departments and agencies of the government. Present recruiting for these men is a hit-or-miss affair carried on at the departmental, presidential, congressional, and national party levels.

No greater service could be performed by the national party committees, especially by their regional representatives, than to compile a continuing roster of good people in and out of the party organization for these strategic jobs. Selecting the right men, of course, would have to be done ultimately by the President in a full understanding of state and congressional party interests.

But the job is too important not to be undertaken systematically, and the national committees should assist in this vital activity.

### THE TRADITIONAL CONFLICTS

The contention that a political shift is inevitable in this country and that changes, such as those advocated above, in the traditional national party arrangements are now possible rests on a theory of politics supported by empirical evidence.

The theory, borrowed intact from Professor E. E. Schattschneider, is that politics is basically concerned with the expression and resolution of conflict. The relevant corollary of the theory is that if the nature of social conflict changes, either political institutions must adjust in order to reflect the new social impulses or society suffers the penalties which inertia and impairment of function exact. In a democratic society, the atmosphere is conducive to adjustment.

The parties historically have performed a variety of very valuable functions in American society. They have been functions of accommodation, compromise, and the peaceful transmission of power. Only rarely have the parties been concerned with insuring coherence of program or responsible power in the carrying out of program. Their lack of interest in national policies backed by national political power can be largely explained by the nature of the social conflicts with which they have had to deal.

### NEW AND OLD SETTLERS

One of the perennial conflicts in American history has been that between new and old settlers.

Historically, as one generation became settled and adjusted, it tended to look hostilely at new arrivals, particularly if the newcomers were from a different part of the old world, spoke a different language, or had a different religion. In the fourteen years before World War I, immigration rose to a peak of a million a year. In contrast to the nineteenth century immigration, the largest part of this million came from southern and eastern Europe: Italy, Poland, Russia, Hungary, Greece. Each group in turn has pursued the American dream; each in turn has found the upward ladder wobbly, and at times sticky. Part of the glory of our traditional party system has been that when other ladders were removed the political ladder was almost always open. But many crowded on the ladder at once; and as some of those below overtook those on the higher rungs, conflict was inevitable.

### SECTIONS AND CLASSES

If the new and the old have warred, so have sections and classes. In the early days it was the frontier farmer against the commercial and financial interests of the seaboard.

As the continent expanded, other regional economic interests developed to complicate the conflict: commodity interests—tobacco, cotton, wheat, corn, sheep, minerals, fish, cattle, fruit, dairy products, oil, and an infinite variety of regional manufacturing interests. Some wanted high tariffs, some wanted low; some wanted federal aid, some wanted no federal interference of any kind. For years these regional interests were dominant forces in American politics.

For a brief period during the Jacksonian era, the Whig Party forged an uneasy upper-class national alliance which attempted to bind regional interests into a national party. But the localized economic and social pressures were too strong, and the

Whigs disintegrated in 1852. It was the parochialism of the economic and social interests of the South before the Civil War that made the irrepressible conflict irrepressible. After the war, a relatively nationwide two-party system came into being, but, as regional pressures erupted, the system became increasingly unstable. By 1896 the "solid Democratic South" had become a fixed political reality, and it was more than matched by a "solid Republican North" which effectively dominated American politics, except in the Wilsonian period, for a generation.

The remnants of these and other regional struggles are still with us, especially in the Congress, but they have been complicated—sometimes modified, sometimes egregiously promoted—by far-ranging class conflicts between rich and poor, debtor and creditor, capital and labor, small farmers and big farmers.

THE NEGRO ISSUE

The Negro issue has occupied a central place in the development of the national party organizations and in the formation of political alliances. Because the issue seemed until recently a "Southern" problem, the Democratic Party as the more national of the two parties had to live a precarious existence astride a two-headed donkey. It survived by promising the Presidency to the North and the Congress to the South. The Republican Party, on the other hand, as a party operating effectively only in the North, was able to strike a bargain with southern Democrats which linked white supremacy and business supremacy in the policy labyrinths of the Congress. The bargain clouded the image of each party and put largely irresponsible power over policy in the hands of a Southern Democratic–Northern Republican coalition, buttressed by seniority and hallowed by carefully designed rules. None of this would have happened if the parties had not had to juggle the Negro issue. It has been the single most useful device of the economic conservatives to keep the political parties from becoming coherent instruments of majority rule.

## The Changes In The Conflicts

The national parties have become what they are because of these historical conflicts which they have had to settle, hide, or gloss

17

over. In some cases they have been the master brokers between rich and poor, country and city, butter and oleo, capital and labor, Italian and Irish, new and old. At other times, they have hidden certain conflicts in order to satisfy powerful economic interests which have stood to gain by exploiting conflict locally and disguising it nationally.

But what happens when the conditions of conflict change? For they are changing, and rapidly, in the United States.

THE SOCIAL CHANGES

Take the struggle between the old and the new. We used to be able to tell the difference between old and new settlers by their accent, or dress, or occupational level. But we are fuller of hundred-per-cent Americans every day and are rapidly reaching the time when nationality politics will be as anachronistic as the trolley car. Samuel Lubell has set the beginning of the end of this traditional conflict in the late thirties, with the coming of age of those whose parents and grandparents had arrived in the great immigration surge at the turn of this century. Matters which once split us and made us fearful are now absorbed almost without question as our population becomes increasingly homogenized.

Or take sectional and class conflict. The heart has been cut out of sectionalism by vast changes in technology and communications which have dispersed industry and revolutionized agriculture. Where are the one-crop "Cotton Ed" Smiths of a few years back? The fact is that there are precious few one-crop areas left in America. And even where there are, as in some of the great agricultural regions of the Great Plains, technology is bringing a revolution of another kind. In the last five years almost four million people have left the farm. The forecast for reapportionment of congressional seats after the 1960 census suggests a dramatic decrease in rural representation in the United States Congress, and this trend will continue as the rise in population throws more and more people into metropolitan areas, and as the effects of *Baker* v. *Carr* become apparent.

The movement in urban politics tends to be toward class rather than regional politics. But even class politics has changed. It is among other things national industry against highly bu-

reaucratized and well-paid national labor. Senator Barry Gold-
water of Arizona is not a regional figure. In the congressional
elections of 1958, national giants contended in that sparsely
populated desert state, and for national stakes.

What bothers the auto worker in Detroit bothers the auto
worker in Los Angeles. What worries the businessman in Chicago
worries his competitor in Boston. With transcontinental jet
planes, the political or labor or industrial leader whose home is
in San Francisco is almost more accessible to his counterpart in
New York than is a train traveler from Boston; and, in any case,
distance has been obliterated by electricity, electronics, and the
direct-dial telephone.

And what is happening to the Negro issue? It, too, is becoming nationalized. The Negroes' locust-like migration to
northern metropolitan centers may have brought new problems
to city governments, but it has aroused a critical competition between the two major parties in the North and West to capture the
Negro vote. In heavily populated, evenly divided states, a bloc
shift of a few votes can mean thirty or forty electoral college
votes for a presidential candidate.

Perhaps more than any one other factor, the northern migration of the Negro is working tremendous transformations in
our political life. The South no longer can exercise a veto in
either presidential convention. For, in more than sixty congressional districts in the North and West, the Negro holds the
political balance of power if he decides to bloc-vote; and in the
South his political power is likely to increase steadily despite
the present tensions.

THE PARTY CHANGES

The shifts in the nature of the conflicts are reflected in the
changes that are already taking place in our party system:

1. The number of one-party states and one-party congressional districts is dramatically declining.

2. The permanent staffs of the national party committees
and the variety of committee functions have grown greatly during the past decade.

3. Almost unnoticed, a revolution has occurred in the "na-
tionalization" of off-year senatorial and congressional campaigns.

In 1954, when both the President and the titular leader of the Democrats actively campaigned in their parties' congressional elections, both the newspapers and the voters seemed to accept the fact that it was perfectly all right for the executive wings of the parties to interest themselves actively in the outcome of the legislative contests. In 1958, both national committees sent out representatives to help develop party strength in various regions and to give services to local campaigns. In 1962, President Kennedy and key executive branch personnel campaigned vigorously for a Democratic Congress until the Cuban crisis interfered.

4. Since 1937, the Presidents have met regularly with party leaders in the Congress on matters of legislative priority and strategy. This has elevated the prestige and power of these men, particularly on matters of foreign policy and national defense.

5. The creation of the Democratic Advisory Council and the recent appearance of embryonic Republican counterparts show a new concern in both parties for clarifying the party image.

### THE CONCLUSION

This far from exhaustive list of the responses of our political system to nationalizing forces represents only the beginnings of adaptation and adjustment. Our basic political institutions, and their relationships to each other and to the public, are in a state of flux. If we want a political system designed to give full play to America's political energies and to hold them within bounds set by a popular majority, we are obligated to modify the system still further.

The reforms outlined in these pages will not obviate America's continuing need for personal force and political virtuosity in the office of the Presidency and in top positions in the Congress. Nor will these or any other party reforms dispel the terrifying military, diplomatic, and social problems of our age. But they will help the parties toward stronger leadership in a more responsible framework than has been traditional. To paraphrase Emerson, they can help us to perceive the terror of life and to man ourselves to face it. In this apocalyptic age, can we ask for greater service from our political parties? We must not ask for less.

EDWARD C. BANFIELD

•

# IN DEFENSE OF THE
# AMERICAN PARTY SYSTEM

The American party system has been criticized on four main grounds: (1) The parties do not offer the electorate a choice in terms of fundamental principles; their platforms are very similar and mean next to nothing; (2) they cannot discipline those whom they elect, and therefore they cannot carry their platforms into effect; (3) they are held together and motivated less by political principle than by desire for personal, often material, gain, and by sectional and ethnic loyalties; consequently party politics is personal and parochial; and (4) their structure is such that they cannot correctly represent the opinion of the electorate; in much of the country there is in effect only one party, and everywhere large contributors and special interests exercise undue influence within the party.[1]

These criticisms may be summarized by saying that the structure and operation of the parties do not accord with the

[1] These criticisms are made, for example, by the French political scientist, Maurice Duverger, in *Political Parties* (New York: Wiley, 1954). For similar criticisms by Americans, see especially Committee on Political Parties of the American Political Science Association, *Toward a More Responsible Two-Party System* (New York: Rinehart, 1950), and E. E. Schattschneider, *Party Government* (New York: Farrar & Rinehart, 1942). Criticisms of American parties are summarized and analyzed in Austin Ranney, *The Doctrine of Responsible Party Government* (Urbana: University of Illinois Press, 1954). Defenses of the American party system include A. Lawrence Lowell, *Essays on Government* (Boston: Houghton Mifflin, 1889), Chs. I, II; Arthur N. Holcombe, *The Political Parties of Today* (New York: Harper, 1925); and *Our More Perfect Union* (Cambridge: Harvard University Press, 1950); Pendleton Herring, *The Politics of Democracy* (New York: Norton, 1940); and Herbert Agar, *The Price of Union* (Boston: Houghton Mifflin, 1950).

theory of democracy or, more precisely, with that theory of it which says that everyone should have a vote, that every vote should be given exactly the same weight, and that the majority should rule.

"It is a serious matter," says Maurice Duverger, a French political scientist who considers American party organization "archaic" and "undemocratic," "that the greatest nation in the world, which is assuming responsibilities on a world-wide scale, should be based on a party system entirely directed towards very narrow local horizons."[2] He and other critics of the American party system do not, however, base their criticisms on the performance of the American government. They are concerned about procedures, not results. They ask whether the structure and operation of the parties is consistent with the logic of democracy, not whether the party system produces—and maintains —a good society, meaning, among other things, one in which desirable human types flourish, the rights of individuals are respected, and matters affecting the common good are decided, as nearly as possible, by reasonable discussion.[3]

If they were to evaluate the party system on the basis of results, they would have to conclude that on the whole it is a good one. It has played an important part (no one can say how important, of course, for innumerable causal forces have been at work along with it) in the production of a society which, despite all its faults, is as near to being a good one as any and nearer by far than most; it has provided governments which, by the standards appropriate to apply to governments, have been humane and, in some crises, bold and enterprising; it has done relatively little to impede economic growth and in some ways has facilitated it; except for the Civil War, when it was, as Henry Jones Ford said, "the last bond of union to give way,"[4] it has tended to check violence, moderate conflict, and narrow the cleavages within the society; it has never produced, or very seriously threatened to produce, either mob rule or tyranny, and

[2] *Op. cit.*, p. 53.

[3] The report of the Committee on Parties of the American Political Science Association, cited above, discusses the "effectiveness" of parties entirely in terms of procedure. Duverger does the same.

[4] Henry Jones Ford, *The Rise and Growth of American Politics* (New York: Macmillan, 1900), p. 303.

it has shown a marvelous ability to adapt to changing circumstances.

Not only has the American party system produced good results, it has produced better ones than have been produced almost anywhere else by other systems. Anyone who reflects on recent history must be struck by the following paradox: those party systems that have been most democratic in structure and procedure have proved least able to maintain democracy; those that have been most undemocratic in structure and procedure—conspicuously those of the United States and Britain—have proved to be the bulwarks of democracy and of civilization.

This paper explores this paradox. It maintains that there is an inherent antagonism between "democracy of procedure" and "production of, and maintenance of, a good society"; that some defects of procedure are indispensable conditions of success from the standpoint of results, and that what the critics call the "archaic" character of the American party system is a very small price to pay for government that can be relied upon to balance satisfactorily the several conflicting ends that must be served.

### DIFFICULTIES IN PLANNING CHANGE

Before entering into these matters, it may be well to remind the reader how difficult is the problem of planning social change.

Social relationships constitute systems: they are mutually related in such a manner that a change in one tends to produce changes in all of the others. If we change the party system in one respect, even a seemingly trivial one, we are likely to set in motion a succession of changes which will not come to an end until the whole system has been changed. The party system, moreover, is an element of a larger political system and of a social system. A small change in the structure or operation of parties may have important consequences for, say, the family, religion, or the business firm.

The changes that we intend when making a reform, if they occur at all, are always accompanied by others that we do not intend. These others may occur at points in the system far removed from the one where the change was initiated and be apparently unrelated to it. Commonly changes produced indirectly and unintentionally turn out to be much more important than the ones that were sought. This is a fact that is seldom fully taken into account. Those who support a particular reform are often indifferent to its consequences for values that they either do not share or consider subordinate. Even those who feel obliged to take a wide range of values into account do not usually try very hard to anticipate the indirect consequences of reforms—often for a very good reason: the complexity of the social system makes the attempt implausible. Usually we take it on faith that the consequences we get by intention justify the risk we take of incurring others that we do not intend or want. Since these others are seldom recognized as consequences of our action at all (they either go unnoticed or seem to have "just happened"), the basis of our faith is not called into question.

No doubt it is a great help to the practical reformer to have tunnel vision. But those who are concerned with the welfare of society as a whole must take the widest perspective possible. They must try to identify all of the consequences that will follow from a reform—the unintended ones no less than the intended, the remote, contingent, and imponderable no less than the immediate, certain, the specifiable. And they must evaluate all of these consequences in the light of a comprehensive system of values.

Those who devise "improvements" to a social system can rarely hope to attain all of their ends; usually they must be prepared to sacrifice some of them to achieve others. This is so because resources are usually limited and also because there are often incompatibilities among ends such that a gain in terms of some necessarily involves a loss in terms of others. The reformer must therefore economize. He must be able to assign priorities to all ends in such a way that he can tell how much of each to sacrifice for how much of others, on various assumptions as to "supply."

The critics of the party system tend to value democratic procedure for its own sake, that is, apart from the results it produces. There is no reason why they should not do so. But they are in error when they do not recognize that other values of equal or greater importance are often in conflict with democratic procedure, and that when they are, some sacrifice of it is essential in order to serve the other values adequately. If they faced up to the necessity of assigning priorities among all of the relevant ends, they would not, it is safe to say, put "democratic procedure" first. Probably they, and most Americans, would order the ends as follows:

1. The party system must above all else provide governments having the will and capacity to preserve the society and to protect its members. Any sacrifice in other ends ought to be accepted if it is indispensable to securing this end.

2. The party system must insure periodic opportunity to change the government by free elections. Any sacrifice of other ends (except the one above) ought to be accepted if it is indispensable to securing this one.

3. The party system should promote the welfare of the people. By "welfare" is meant some combination of two kinds of values: "principles," what is thought to be good for the society, described in rather general terms, and "interests," the ends individuals and groups seek to attain for their own good, as distinguished from that of the society. The party system should produce governments that assert the supremacy of principles over interests in some matters; in others it should allow interests to prevail and should facilitate the competitive exercise of influence.

4. The party system should moderate and restrain such conflict as would threaten the good health of the society. Other conflict it should not discourage.

5. The party system should promote and exemplify democracy, meaning reasonable discussion of matters affecting the common good in which every voice is heard.

These ends have been listed in what most Americans would probably consider a descending order of importance. In devising a party system, we ought not to try to serve fully each higher end before serving the one below it at all. The first two ends are exceptions to this rule, however: each of them must be attained even if the others are not served at all. With respect to the remaining three, the problem is to achieve a proper balance—one such that no reallocation from one end to another would add to the sum of value.

Finally, we must realize that we can rarely make important social changes by intention. The most we can do is to make such minor changes as may be consistent with, and more or less implied by, the fixed features of the situation in which we are placed. Even to make minor changes in an institution like a political party requires influence of a kind and amount that no group of reformers is likely to have or to be able to acquire. It is idle to propose reforms that are merely desirable. There must also be some possibility of showing, if only in a rough and conjectural way, that they might be carried into effect.

With respect to the American party system, it seems obvious that the crucial features of the situation are all fixed. The size of our country, the class and cultural heterogeneity of our people, the number and variety of their interests, the constitutionally-given fragmentation of formal authority, the wide distribution of power which follows from it, the inveterate taste of Americans for participation in the day-to-day conduct of government when their interests are directly at stake—these are all unalterable features of the situation. Taken together, they mean that the party system can be reformed only within very narrow limits.

## A MODEL PARTY SYSTEM

Let us imagine a system free of the alleged defects of ours. In this model system, every citizen is motivated—highly so—by political principles, not subsidiary ones, but ones having to do with the very basis of the society. (In France and Italy, Duverger says approvingly, political warfare "is not concerned with subsidiary principles but with the very foundations of the state and the nature of the regime."[5]) The electoral system, moreover, is such as to give every side on every issue exactly the weight that its numbers in the population warrant; no group or interest is over- or under-represented ("One's thoughts turn," Duverger says, "to the possibility of a truly scientific democracy, in which parliament would be made up of a true sample of the citizens reproducing on a reduced scale the exact composition of the nation, made up, that is, according to the very methods that are used as a basis for public opinion surveys like the Gallup polls."[6])

Assuming that the society is divided by the usual number of cleavages (e.g., haves versus have-nots, segregationists versus anti-

[5] *Op. cit.*, p. 419.
[6] *Ibid.*, p. 158.

segregationists, isolationists versus internationalists, etc.), the following would result:

1. There would be a great many parties, for no citizen would support a party with which he did not agree fully.

2. The parties would tend to be single-issue ones. If logically unrelated issues (for instance, segregation and isolationism) were linked together in a party program, only those voters would support the party who chanced to be on the same side of all of the linked issues. The number of these voters would decrease as the number of issues so linked increased.

3. Parties would be short-lived. They would come into and pass out of existence with the single issues they were organized to fight.

4. In their election campaigns and propaganda, parties would emphasize their single defining principles. This would tend to widen the cleavages along which the parties were formed.

5. Ideological issues, not practical problems, would constitute the substance of politics.[7]

6. The number of such issues pressing for settlement at any one time (but being incapable of settlement because of their ideological character) would always be more than the system could accommodate.[8]

7. Coalitions of parties would seldom form, and such as did form would be highly unstable. Party leaders would find compromise almost impossible because it would lead to loss of highly principled supporters.

8. Coalitions of parties being unstable, governments would also be unstable and therefore lacking in power and decision.

9. Those selected for positions of political leadership would tend to be ideologues skilled in party dialectics and symbolizing the party and its positions. Practical men, especially those with a talent for compromise and those symbolizing qualities common to the whole society, would be excluded from politics.

10. Matters having no ideological significance (a category

[7] In France, according to Siegfried, "every argument becomes a matter of principle; the practical results are relegated to second place." André Siegfried, "Stable Instability in France," *Foreign Affairs*, XXXIV (April 1956), 395.

[8] According to Siegfried: "The difficulty is that too many questions of fundamental importance on which the various parties have cause to disagree have come up for decision at one time." *Ibid.*, p. 399.

that includes most local issues) would either be endowed with a spurious one or else would be left outside the sphere of politics altogether.[9]

These points should suffice to show that a system with a perfectly democratic structure would not produce results acceptable in terms of the criteria listed above.

Now let us introduce into the model system one of the alleged defects which the critics find most objectionable in the American party system. Let us suppose that at least half of the electorate is prevailed upon to exchange its vote in matters of fundamental principle for advantages that have nothing to do with principle, especially private profit, sectional gain, and nationality "recognition."

One effect of this would be to reduce greatly the intensity of ideological conflict and to make political life more stable and conservative. This, in fact, seems to be what happened when American parties first came into being. John Adams tells in his diary how in 1794 "ten thousand people in the streets of Philadelphia, day after day, threatened to drag Washington out of his house and effect a revolution in the government, or compel it to declare war in favor of the French Revolution and against England."[10] After parties had been organized, however, patronage took the place of ideological fervor. "The clubs of the social revolutionists which had sprung up in the cities, blazing with incendiary ideas caught from the French Revolution," Henry Jones Ford says, "were converted into party workers, and their behavior was moderated by considerations of party interest."[11]

Another effect would be to encourage the formation of a few (probably two) stable parties. These might begin as alliances among the profit-minded, the sectional-minded, and the nationality-minded, but to attract support from principled voters the parties would have to seem to stand for something—indeed,

[9] In France, Luethy says, "politics," which deals with ideological matters, and the "state," i.e., the bureaucracy, which deals with practical ones, function "in watertight compartments" with the consequence that French democracy is an amalgam of absolutist administration on the one hand and of anarchy, tumultuous or latent, on the other. Herbert Luethy, *France Against Herself* (New York: Meridian Books, 1957), p. 61. On this see also Siegfried, *op. cit., p.* 399.

[10] Quoted by Henry Jones Ford, *op. cit.,* p. 125.

[11] *Ibid.,* p. 144.

for anything and everything. Since no faction of them could hope to win an election by itself, principled voters would attach themselves to those parties that they found least objectionable. The parties would develop corporate identities and mystiques; principled voters would then subordinate their differences out of "loyalty" to the party and in response to its demands for "regularity." Competition for middle-of-the-road support would cause the parties to offer very similar programs. This competition might lead to there being only two parties, but this result would probably be insured by introducing another supposed defect into the system: a principle of representation (single-member districts and plurality voting) which, by letting the winner take all, would force small parties to join large ones in order to have some chance of winning.

In one way or another, the "defects" of the system would tend to produce these consequences—consequences which have in fact been produced in the United States:

1. A strong and stable government would be possible. The country would be governed by the party that won the election, or (given the particular complexities of the American system) by two closely similar parties engaged in give-and-take and, therefore, in a sense constituting one party under two names.

2. There would be a high degree of continuity between administrations elected from different parties. Elections would not shake the nation to its foundations because the competing parties would be fundamentally in agreement. Agreement would be so built in by countless compromises within the parties (each of which would be under the necessity of attracting middle-of-the-road support) that a change of party would seldom entail complete reversal of policy in an important matter.

3. There would exist many substructures of power that would be largely or wholly impervious to the influence of political principle or ideology. "Machines"—party organizations of the profit-minded, the sectional-minded, and the nationality-minded—would not be inclined to offer pie in the sky or to stir the emotions of the masses because they could count upon getting their votes in other ways. These essentially apolitical centers of power would therefore exert a stabilizing and conservative influence throughout the political system. By making busi-

nesslike deals with the leaders of the "machines," the President could sometimes buy freedom to do as he thought best in matters of principle.

4. The diversity of the principles and the multiplicity of the interests within the party would be another source of strength to the leader elected from it. He could afford to offend some elements of the party on any particular question because there would be enough other elements unaffected (or even gratified) to assure his position. The more fragmented his party, the less attention he would have to pay to any one fragment of it.

5. The assertion of interests (as distinguished from principles) would be encouraged. The profit-minded, the sectional-minded, and the nationality-minded would in effect give up representation on matters of principle in order to get it on matters involving their interests. Thus two different systems of representation would work simultaneously. The party leader would act as a trustee, disregarding interests in favor of principles ("Congress represents locality, the President represents the nation," Ford wrote in 1898.[12]) Meanwhile legislators dependent on machines and, in general, on profit-minded, sectional-minded, and nationality-minded voters would act as agents of interests. The trustee of principles (the President) and the agents of interests (Congressmen) would of necessity bargain with each other; by allowing the agents of interests some successes—but only in this way—the trustee of principles could win their support in the matters he considered most important. Thus, there would be achieved that balancing of interests and of interests against principles (the most important principles usually being vindicated) that a good party system should produce.

6. The formation of deep cleavages would nevertheless be discouraged. The competition of the parties for the middle-of-the-road vote; their tendency to select practical men of wide popular appeal, rather than ideologues, for positions of leadership; and the definition of the politicians' task as being that of finding the terms on which people who disagree will work to-

[12] *Ibid.*, p. 187. For a recent brilliant account of how the two systems of representation work, see Willmoore Kendall, "The Two Majorities," *Midwest Journal of Political Science*, IV, No. 4 (November 1960), 317–345.

gether, rather than that of sharpening ideological points—these would all be unifying tendencies.

Some critics of the American party system have attributed its alleged defects to the absence of class consciousness in our society. No doubt there is some truth in this. But causality may run the other way also. We may be lacking in class consciousness because our politicians are prevented by the nature of the party system from popularizing the rhetoric of the class struggle; the party system actually induces the voter to forgo the allurements of principle and ideology by offering him things he values more: e.g., personal profit, sectional advantage, and nationality "recognition."[13]

In those countries where the voter expresses at the polls his ideology rather than his interests, he may do so not from choice but because the party system leaves him no alternative. In such countries, class warfare may be the principal subject-matter of politics simply because matters of greater importance to the voters are not at stake.

Experience in the underdeveloped areas seems to bear out the claim that certain "defects" in a party system may be essential to good government. The transplanted "defects" of the American party system are among the factors that have made the Philippines the most democratic country in Southeast Asia. According to Professor Lucian W. Pye:

> . . . the image of leadership that evolved in the Philippines was clearly that of the politician who looked after the particular interests of voters. Elsewhere the pattern of the Western impact under colonialism gave emphasis to the role of the rational administrator who apparently

[13] ". . . in coordinating the various elements of the populations for political purposes," Ford says, "party organization tends at the same time to fuse them into one mass of citizenship, pervaded by a common order of ideas and sentiments, and actuated by the same class of motives. This is probably the secret of the powerful solvent influence which American civilization exerts upon the enormous deposits of alien population thrown upon this country by the torrent of emigration. Racial and religious antipathies, which present the most threatening problems to countries governed upon parliamentary principles, melt with amazing rapidity in the warm flow of a party spirit which is constantly demanding, and is able to reward the subordination of local and particular interests to national purposes." (*Op. cit.*, pp. 306–307.)

operated according to the principles of efficiency and who was not supposed to be influenced by political pressures within the society. Consequently, when the politicians emerged in these societies, they tended to become the champions of nationalistic ideologies and even the enemies of the rational administrators.[14]

In the Philippines, as at home, our party system has had the defects of its virtues—and the virtues of its defects. On the one hand, Pye says, the Philippines have never had an efficient administrative machinery, and the demand for higher standards of personal integrity among their public officials is reminiscent of the muckraking era of American politics; on the other hand, "the Philippine electorate seems to recognize that the most fundamental question in politics is who is going to control the government, and thus, while the parties have not had to expend much effort in trying to distinguish themselves ideologically from each other, the expenditures of money on political campaigns in the Philippines are probably the highest in proportion to per capita income of any country in the world."[15]

## MAKING PARTIES "RESPONSIBLE"

Some think that the American party system can be reformed without changing its nature essentially. Several years ago, a Committee on Parties of the American Political Science Association proposed making certain "readjustments" in the structure and operation of the party system to eliminate its "defects." These readjustments, the Committee said, would give the electorate "a proper range of choice between alternatives" in the form of programs to which the parties would be committed and which they would have sufficient internal cohesion to carry into effect. Thus, the two-party system would be made more "responsible."[16]

What this means is not at all clear. "Responsibility" here seems to be a synonym for accountability, that is, the condition of being subject to being called to account and made to take

[14] Lucian W. Pye, "The Politics of Southeast Asia," in G. Almond and J. Coleman (eds.), *The Politics of the Developing Areas* (Princeton, N.J.: Princeton University Press, 1960), p. 97. Copyright © 1960 by Princeton University Press.

[15] *Ibid.*, pp. 123 and 126.

[16] See the Committee Report, *op. cit.*, pp. 1 and 85.

corrective action in response to criticism. In the case of a party, this can mean nothing except going before an electorate, and in this sense all parties are by definition responsible. "Responsibility" can have no other meaning in this context; as William Graham Sumner remarked, "a party is an abstraction; it cannot be held responsible or punished; if it is deprived of power it fades into thin air and the men who composed it, especially those who did the mischief and needed discipline, quickly reappear in the new majority."[17]

Leaving aside both the question of what "responsibility" means when applied to a party and the more important one of whether as a matter of practical politics such "readjustments" could be made, let us consider how the political system would probably be affected by the changes proposed.

The hope that the two-party system might be made to offer a choice between distinct alternatives is illusory for at least two reasons. One is that a party which does not move to the middle of the road to compete for votes condemns itself to defeat and eventually, if it does not change its ways, to destruction. But even if this were not the case, the parties could not present the electorate with what reformers think of as "a valid choice." The reason is that the issues in our national life are such that there does not exist any one grand principle by which the electorate could be divided into two camps such that every voter in each camp would be on the "same" side of all issues. The idea of "left" and "right" is as close as we come to having such a grand principle, and it has little or no application to many issues.[18] The logic of "left" and "right" does not, for example, imply opposite or even different positions on (for example) foreign policy, civil liberties, or farm subsidies. Without a grand principle which will make unities—opposed unities—of the party programs, the electorate cannot be offered "a valid choice." A

[17] William Graham Sumner, *The Challenge of Facts* (New Haven, Conn.: Yale University Press, 1914), pp. 271–272).

[18] One can imagine a set of symbols connected with a diffuse ideology dividing the society into two camps, and to a certain extent this exists. But it is hard to see in what sense this would present the electorate with "a valid choice." In other words, the existence of a body of nonsense which is treated as if it were a grand principle ought not to be regarded by reasonable critics of the party system as equivalent to the grand principle itself.

choice between two market baskets, each of which contains an assortment of unrelated items, some of which are liked and some of which are disliked, is not a "valid" choice in the same sense that a choice between two market baskets, each of which contains items that "belong together" is a "valid" one. In the American party system, most items are logically unrelated. This being so, "valid" choice would become possible only if the number of parties was increased to allow each party to stand for items that *were* logically related, if one issue became important to the exclusion of all of the others, or if, by the elaboration of myth and ideology, pseudo-logical relations were established among items.

The hope that the parties might commit themselves to carry out their programs is also illusory. A party could do this only if its leaders were able to tell the President and the party members in Congress what to do, and could discipline them if they failed to do it. Therefore, unless, like the Russians, we were to have two sets of national leaders, one in governmental office and another much more important one in party office, it would be necessary for our elected leaders—in effect, the President, since only he and the Vice President are elected by the whole nation —to control the Congressmen and Senators of their party. This would be possible only if the President could deny re-election to members of Congress who did not support the party program. Thus, instead of merely bringing forward and electing candidates, as they do now, "responsible" parties would have to govern the country. We would have a parliamentary system with the President in a position somewhat like that of the British Prime Minister, except (a very important difference) that, not being a part of the legislature, he could not use it as a vehicle through which to exert his leadership.[19] The legislature would in fact have no function at all.

This great shift of power to the President would remedy

[19] The Prime Minister is the leader of his party outside as well as inside Parliament. Party leaders who are not also members of Parliament take no part in the running of the government, as the late Professor Harold Laski discovered when, as a leader of the Labour Party, he presumed to give advice to Prime Minister Attlee. The party leaders discipline their followers by threatening to deprive them of renomination; accordingly most members of the House are "backbenchers" who participate in its affairs only as audience, and the function of the House as a whole is to criticize and advise the leaders of the majority party.

another "defect" in the party system: its receptivity to the demands of interest groups.[20] With the President in full control of Congress, logrolling would cease or virtually cease. It would do so because no one could any longer make the President pay a price for assistance in getting legislation passed; the traders who now sell their bits and pieces of power to the highest bidders would have to lower their prices and would probably go out of business. With their opportunities for exercising influence vastly reduced, interest groups would be less enterprising both in their efforts to anticipate the effects of governmental action and in bringing their views to the attention of the policy makers.

The making of policy would thus pass largely into the hands of technical experts within the majority party, the White House, and the executive departments. These would be mindful of principles and impatient of interests. They would endeavor to make "coherent" policies, meaning, presumably, policies not based on compromise.[21] In all important matters, however, "the public interest" would prove an insufficient guide; the experts, when confronted with the necessity of choosing between alternatives that were equally in the public interest—that is, when no authoritative, ultimate criterion of choice existed for them to apply—would by the very necessities of the case have to balance the competing values as best they could, which means that they would have to fall back upon their personal tastes or professional biases.[22] Thus they would do badly (but in the name of "impartial administration") what is now done reasonably well by the political process.

The destruction of political traders and of local centers of power would mean also that the President's power would derive from somewhat different sources than at present. Instead of relying upon logrolling and patronage to get the votes he would need in Congress, he would have to rely upon direct appeals to the electorate. To some extent he might manipulate the electorate by charm and personality; TV and the arts of Madison

---

[20] Cf. Report of the Committee on Parties, *op. cit.*, pp. 19–20.
[21] *Ibid.*, p. 19.
[22] This argument is developed in E. C. Banfield, *Political Influence* (Glencoe, Ill.: Free Press, 1961), Ch. 12.

Avenue would become more important in politics. But in order to get elected he would have to depend also, and to a greater extent, upon appeals to political principle or ideology. Whereas the political trader maintains his control by giving and withholding favors to individuals (a circumstance which makes his control both dependable in its operation and cheap), the President would have to maintain *his* by the uncertain and costly expedient of offering to whole classes of people—the farmer, the aged, the home owner, and so on—advantages that they would have only at each other's expense. If charm and the promise of "something for everybody" did not yield the amount of power he required to govern the country, the President might find it necessary to exploit whatever antagonisms within the society might be made to yield more power. Class and ethnic differences might in this event serve somewhat the same function as logrolling and patronage do now. Mayor LaGuardia, for example, depended for power upon direct, personal appeal to the voters rather than upon organization. His charm and his support of "liberal" programs are well remembered. But it should not be forgotten that he depended also upon exploitation of ethnic loyalties and antipathies. According to Robert Moses,

> It must be admitted that in exploiting racial and religious prejudices LaGuardia could run circles around the bosses he despised and derided. When it came to raking ashes of Old World hates, warming ancient grudges, waving the bloody shirt, tuning the ear to ancestral voices, he could easily out-demagogue the demagogues. And for what purpose? To redress old wrongs abroad? To combat foreign levy or malice domestic? To produce peace on the Danube, the Nile, the Jordan? Not on your tintype. Fiorello LaGuardia knew better. He knew that the aim of the rabble rousers is simply to shoo into office for entirely extraneous, illogical and even silly reasons the municipal officials who clean city streets, teach in schools, protect, house and keep healthy, strong and happy millions of people crowded together here.[23]

That a President might rely more upon appeals to political principle does not at all mean that better judgments or results would follow. For the discussion of principles would probably

[23] Robert Moses, *LaGuardia: A Salute and a Memoir* (New York: Simon & Schuster, 1957), pp. 37–38. Copyright © 1957 by Simon & Schuster.

not be *serious;* it would be for the purpose of securing popular interest and consent, not of finding a wise or right course of action. As long ago as 1886, Sir Henry Sumner Maine observed that democracy was tending toward government by salesmanship. Party and corruption had in the past always been relied upon to bring men under civil discipline, he said, but now a third expedient had been discovered:

> This is generalization, the trick of rapidly framing, and confidently uttering, general propositions on political subjects. . . . General formulas, which can be seen on examination to have been arrived at by attending only to particulars few, trivial or irrelevant, are turned out in as much profusion as if they dropped from an intellectual machine; and debates in the House of Commons may be constantly read, which consisted wholly in the exchange of weak generalities and strong personalities. On a pure Democracy this class of general formulas has a prodigious effect. Crowds of men can be got to assent to general statements, clothed in striking language, but unverified and perhaps incapable of verification; and thus there is formed a sort of sham and pretence of concurrent opinion. There has been a loose acquiescence in a vague proposition, and then the People, whose voice is the voice of God, is assumed to have spoken.[24]

Efforts to create "levity of assent," as Maine called it, will become more important in our politics to the extent that other means of bringing men under civil discipline are given up or lost.

## THE DANGER OF MEDDLING

A political system is an accident. It is an accumulation of habits, customs, prejudices, and principles that have survived a long process of trial and error and of ceaseless response to changing circumstance. If the system works well on the whole, it is a lucky accident—the luckiest, indeed, that can befall a society, for all of the institutions of the society, and thus its entire character and that of the human types formed within it, depend ultimately upon the government and the political order.

---

[24] Sir Henry Sumner Maine, *Popular Government* (New York: Henry Holt, 1886), pp. 106–108.

## Edward C. Banfield

To meddle with the structure and operation of a successful political system is therefore the greatest foolishness that men are capable of. Because the system is intricate beyond comprehension, the chance of improving it in the ways intended is slight, whereas the danger of disturbing its working and of setting off a succession of unwanted effects that will extend throughout the whole society is great.

Democracy must always meddle, however. An immanent logic impels it to self-reform, and if other forces do not prevent, it must sooner or later reform itself out of existence.[25]

The logic of this is as follows. The ideal of democracy legitimates only such power as arises out of reasonable discussion about the common good in which all participate. Power that comes into being in any other way (e.g., by corruption, logrolling, appeals to sentiment or prejudice, the exercise of charm or charisma, "hasty generalization," terror, etc.) is radically undemocratic, and people inspired by the democratic ideal will therefore endeavor to eliminate it by destroying, or reforming, whatever practices or institutions give rise to it.

No society, however, can be governed *solely* by reasonable discussion about the common good; even in a society of angels there might be disagreement about what the common good requires in the concrete case.[26] In most societies, far more power is needed to maintain civil discipline and protect the society from its enemies than can be got simply by reasonable discussion about the common good. Therefore the logical culmination of democratic reform, viz., the elimination of all undemocratic sources of power, would render government—and therefore the preservation of the society—impossible. Democratic reform can never reach this point, of course, because, before reaching it, democracy itself would be destroyed and the impetus to further reform removed.

So far as it does succeed, however, the tendency of democratic reform is to reduce the power available for government. Such loss of power as occurs from the elimination of undemo-

[25] For data and analysis pertinent to the discussion that follows, see James Q. Wilson, *The Amateur Democrat* (Chicago: University of Chicago Press, 1962).
[26] See Yves R. Simon, *The Philosophy of Democratic Government* (Chicago: University of Chicago Press, 1951), Ch. 1.

cratic sources of it will seldom be offset by increases in power of the kind that arises from reasonable discussion about the common good. Since there is a point beyond which no increase in democratic power is possible (the capacity of a society to engage in reasonable discussion about the common good being limited), reform, if carried far enough, must finally reduce the quantity of power.

There is, then, a danger that reform will chip away the foundations of power upon which the society rests. But this is not the only danger. A greater one, probably, is that in making some forms of undemocratic power less plentiful, reform may make others more plentiful, and by so doing set off changes that will ramify throughout the political system, changing its character completely. If, for example, politicians cannot get power by the methods of the machine (corruption, favor-giving, and patronage), they may get it by other methods, such as charm, salesmanship, and "hasty generalization." The new methods may be better than the old by most standards (they cannot, of course, be better by the standard of democracy, according to which *all* power not arising from reasonable discussion about the common good is absolutely illegitimate); but even if they are better, the new methods may not serve as well as the old, or may not serve at all, in maintaining an effective political system and a good society.

Reform is, of course, far from being the only force at work. Compared to the other forces, some of which tend to produce competing changes and others of which tend to check all change, reform may be of slight effect. This is certainly true in general of such reform as is sought through formal organizations by people called "reformers." It is much less true of reform in the broader sense of the general view and disposition of "the great body of right-thinking people." This kind of reform is likely to be of pervasive importance in the long run, although its effects are seldom what anyone intended.

Jefferson may have been right in saying that democracy cannot exist without a wide diffusion of knowledge throughout the society. But it may be right also to say that it cannot exist *with* it. For as we become a better and more democratic society, our very goodness and democracy may lead us to destroy goodness and democracy in the effort to increase and perfect them.

WALTER BERNS

•

# REFORM OF THE
# AMERICAN PARTY SYSTEM

> Political systems can to some extent be appraised by the test of
> whether their leading representatives are or are not capable of
> taking decisions in great matters on their merits, in defiance of
> their own interests and often of their best friends.
> —WINSTON CHURCHILL

Political parties, which were once thought to be incompatible
with the American Constitution, are now said to be indispensable to the system of government that has evolved within the
Constitution. Agreement as to their indispensability does not,
however, carry with it an agreement as to how well our parties
are performing the role, the indispensable role, assigned them by
our system, because there is no agreement on what this role is.
In large part, this disagreement on the role of parties derives
from a dispute on the nature of democracy. Whether parties
should be reformed, then, will depend on how well they are
thought to conduce to democracy as this is variously understood.
This paper begins with a brief sketch of the reforms that have
been proposed, continues with a discussion of an argument
against attempting planned changes of any description, and con-
cludes with a consideration of the question whether reforms in
the American party system are in fact needed at this time or in
the foreseeable future.

I

Contemporary debate on the question of reform of the party
system began in 1950 with the publication of the Report of the
Committee on Political Parties of the American Political Science
Association, entitled *Toward a More Responsible Two-Party*

*System.*[1] But the essence of both the criticisms of the American party system and of the reforms suggested in the Report is to be found in a number of studies dating back to Woodrow Wilson's *Congressional Government,* first published in 1885.

Democracy, according to the reformers, is government based on public opinion, which means, in effect, government based on the opinion of the majority. It is unreasonable, however, to expect citizens to participate directly (except to the extent of voting) in the affairs of government in a country the size of the United States, even with the assistance of mass communication devices and public opinion polls; we are thus required to devise a system of majority rule that takes into account the size of the country and of the population. This system is party government. Not only should the parties provide the men and the machinery that, together, fill the offices of government, but the parties should be the vehicles by which public opinion is translated into public policy. This will be accomplished through the establishment of new institutions that facilitate two-way communication on policy matters between the local constituent parties and the national parties, with a view to the formulation of party platforms emphasizing general principles as well as policy statements on national issues. The party elected to office on the basis of a meaningful program, which will embody the political opinions of the majority of the public, has the responsibility for carrying out this program; the other party has the responsibility for opposing the party in office and for standing ready to replace it, if asked to do so by the voters. Effective representation of the majority opinion can be had in the representative assemblies only if the parties are truly representative. Popular rule requires at least two parties (and preferably *only* two parties), each with a meaningful legislative program to which it is committed. Popular rule, majority rule, will be effected ultimately through popular control, and this can exist only when the voters have a clear choice between responsible parties.

According to the reformers, American parties as presently organized are incapable of playing this role. Being composed of men of a wide variety of political opinion, whose primary loyalties are to the dominant groups in their local constituencies

[1] New York: Rinehart & Company, 1950.

41

(whose dominance is likely to be due to their money more than their numbers), with all that this implies, they are incapable of formulating coherent programs, to say nothing of translating programs into legislation. Lacking the discipline that would come from a centralized party committed to a coherent program, individual members of Congress are too accessible to private groups advocating action on behalf of their private interests. In these circumstances, a legislative program can be enacted only with the assistance of members of both parties, with the result that neither party can be held responsible or irresponsible by the voters. As presently constituted, then, the party system prevents democracy, because it prevents the rule of the majority, or control by the majority.

The suggested reforms are laid down with a view to creating centralized *national* parties that possess the institutions to formulate coherent legislative programs, the power to enforce adherence to the programs by their members, and the political power to enact these programs into law. Various changes are proposed to bring such parties into being. One of them is the centralization of party finance, in order to end the reliance of candidates on moneys collected locally. Still another is the proposed consolidation of the various leadership committees in the House and Senate—the steering committees, the policy committees, the committees on committees—into one leadership committee for each party in each house, in order to end the existing dispersion of authority. These new committees would have some responsibility for formulating legislative policy and, what is perhaps more decisive, for making committee assignments, which they would do with a view to abolishing, or at least modifying, the seniority system in Congress, according to which assignments are made on the basis of years of service rather than on agreement with the national party program.[2]

To a greater or lesser extent, what the reformers want is a party system modelled on the one presumed to exist in Britain, where the voters are supposed to be presented with a clear-cut choice between two (or sometimes three) parties, each of which, if elected to office, will possess the political power to govern. The

---

[2] In addition to the Report of the Committee on Political Parties, see Stephen K. Bailey, "Our National Political Parties," pp. 1–20.

reformers are not unaware of the constitutional obstacles to the creation of such a party system in the United States, but they are confident that these obstacles are surmountable. The effect of the separation of powers, for example, can be changed by a party that elects both a President and a Congress in which effective control is in the hands of men of the same political outlook as the President. As for federalism, its ability to prevent the formation of strong national parties rests, at bottom, on geographical differences that give rise to political differences; but when geography no longer generates these differences, and it is losing its ability to do this, one of the major obstacles to the formation of truly national parties will disappear. The proposed changes will merely facilitate the changes that are already taking place.

## II

Party reform has been opposed on at least three distinct grounds, the first of these being the argument that the prescriptions for reform are based on an incorrect analysis of the American as well as the British party system. It was said that the Committee on Political Parties had seriously underestimated the amount of change that has already taken place in American parties and that it had failed to see the considerable party cohesion that now exists. Party, it was claimed, has become an increasingly important factor in congressional voting, and recent years have seen a significant increase in the number of issues on which the two major parties are sharply divided.[3] The Committee was also accused of attributing qualities to the British parties that they do not possess (although there is no argument concerning their cohesion), while ignoring their serious defects.[4]

The second ground of opposition is hostility to utopianism, a position occupied by men who themselves might be accused of cynicism. "It is just possible," one critic said, "that one of party government's requirements, ideological cleavage, is lacking in America for the simple reason most Americans have already answered [the] query, 'What is democracy?' by accepting what

---

[3] Julius Turner, "Responsible Parties: A Dissent from the Floor," *American Political Science Review*, XLV (March, 1951), 143–152.
[4] David Butler, "American Myths About British Parties," *Virginia Quarterly Review*, XXI (1955), 46.

they have. Party-government advocates might heed Arthur Koestler's advice: 'The difference between utopia and a working concern is to know one's limits.' "[5] Another critic accused the Committee of taking off "on a flight to London if not to Utopia, propelling their cargo of hopes along with a burst of suggestions, some precise and some vague. . . ."[6]

The third ground of opposition is occupied by men who attack the reformers, and especially the Committee on Political Parties, in their most vulnerable place: their doctrinairism. As the brief sketch of the reform argument serves to illustrate, the approach of the Committee is almost entirely theoretical.[7] That is, it is less concerned with the policy enacted than it is with the way it is enacted, with procedure rather than substance. Its inspiration is a particular notion of democracy, and its recommendations are made primarily with a view to promoting that kind of democracy, with only an occasional (and never seriously considered) reference to such substantial political matters as the problems of a "precarious and peculiar peace."[8] To justify a rejection of reforms inspired by such considerations, it is sufficient merely to state a preference for another kind of democracy or for the existing system; but some critics go further to argue that, in fact, the existing party system is more compatible with the public interest than the one proposed by the reformers, which has only a theoretical tidiness to recommend it. Whether it is appropriate to go still further, as, in the extreme case, some men do, and condemn all planned change, is questionable.[9] But it would not be the first time that doctrinairism of one extreme has provoked a doctrinairism of the opposite extreme. To condemn

[5] Kenneth G. Olson, in a review of Ranney, *The Doctrine of Responsible Party Government; Its Origins and Present State*, in *The Journal of Politics*, XVII (May, 1955), 299–300.

[6] Clinton Rossiter, *Parties and Politics in America* (Ithaca: Cornell University Press, 1960), p. 179.

[7] This paper will ignore the most theoretical of the party books, Maurice Duverger's *Political Parties*, because Duverger is concerned only with the development of a science of political parties (which is to be a science of party organization) and almost not at all with government. That is to say, his is a book about political science, not politics—in France, Britain, America, or anywhere else.

[8] Report of the Committee on Political Parties, p. 92.

[9] Edward C. Banfield, "In Defense of the American Party System," pp. 38 ff.

all planned change is to condemn the virtue of intelligence, at least with respect to its applicability to the political system itself.

Such an argument reminds us of Edmund Burke, who opposed innovation and change arising out of what he called "metaphysical politics," and said that a sound constitutional system (one founded on prescription) "never was made upon any foregone theory,"[10] the mind-fashioned artifact of "visionary politicians," who looked with "filial reverence on the constitution of [their] country, and never [would] cut it in pieces, and put it into the kettle of any magician, in order to boil it, with the puddle of their compounds, into youth and vigor."[11]

No one is more sanguine of man's ability to establish an ideal political order through planned change than the Marxists, the present-day heirs of the theorists Burke inveighed against in the eighteenth century, who assume that a violent revolution carried on by the lowest class in contemporary society will be followed, eventually and inevitably, by that blessed condition called by Marx, the Realm of Freedom. It was the eighteenth-century version of this doctrinaire confidence in man's wisdom and ability to control events that provoked Burke's statement of the opposite extreme that the "individual is foolish . . . but the species is wise, and, when time is given to it, as a species, it almost always acts right."[12] The element of truth in Burke's position, and the eloquence with which he stated it, might cause us to forget that the species can act only through its individual members, some of whose efforts to reform, and even radically to change, have been singularly successful.

Surely changes in a constitutional order, or in the party system within that order, should be undertaken in a spirit of great sobriety: the same American who said that a little rebellion, now and then, is a good thing, also wrote, on a more sober occasion, that "governments long established should not be changed for light and transient causes." These words of Jefferson's serve to remind us that the American political system is not altogether an accident, but is instead one of the happiest instances of

[10] Edmund Burke, Speech of May 7, 1782, in *Burke's Politics*, ed. Ross J. S. Hoffman and Paul Levack (New York: Alfred A. Knopf, 1949), p. 228.
[11] *Ibid.*, p. 232.
[12] *Ibid.*, p. 227.

planned change ever instituted by man. This success alone compels us to view proposals for change circumspectly, but, at the same time, to consider the possibility that reforms might be required precisely to preserve the system against changes of the magnitude of those of 1776 and 1787. Certainly it would seem advisable to avoid the example of France, where all political reform, indeed, almost all political action, must be preceded by a constitutional upheaval.

To say that the American Constitution is not an accident is not to assert that the system of government that has evolved within its framework is wholly the work of its original framers. The party system alone provides evidence to the contrary. But neither is the party system the product of a blind and inscrutable evolution, or of a History, scrutable or inscrutable. We know that each of the two great parties was brought into being consciously and therefore purposively,[13] and that each of them accomplished the immediate purpose for which it was organized. It is also possible to distinguish particular actions, taken subsequent to their foundation, that affect the character of the parties today—actions of the same order of magnitude as most of the reforms now proposed. One example must suffice.

It is not mere chance that the cities of America are underrepresented in the state legislatures and in the House of Representatives, with the result that today the Senate, formerly the citadel of conservatism, is acknowledged to be more "liberal" than the House (meaning, at least, that the Senate is more likely than the House to be in favor of legislation demanded by the cities). Congress is given the authority to regulate the times, places, and manner of holding elections for representatives, but the actual congressional districts are drawn up in the various state legislatures. These are usually controlled by rural interests, which frequently results in gross malapportionment against the cities;[14] and the efforts of the cities to force the state legislatures to apportion districts equally have failed. This has been true as well of the attempts to use the equity powers of the federal

[13] Harry V. Jaffa, "The Nature and Origin of the American Party System," pp. 59–83.
[14] M. J. Dauer and R. S. Kelsay, "Unrepresentative States," *National Municipal Review*, XLIV (1955), 571.

courts, whose powers would be available and effective were it not for one fact. Beginning with the Apportionment Act of 1929, Congress has omitted a decisive provision, which in the Act of 1911 read as follows: ". . . in each State entitled under this apportionment to more than one Representative, the Representatives to the Sixty-third and each subsequent Congress shall be elected by districts composed of a contiguous and compact territory, and containing as nearly as practicable an equal number of inhabitants. . . ."[15]

Insofar as we are guided by what the Supreme Court itself has said, there can be scarcely any doubt that were this requirement of contiguous, compact, and equal districts a part of federal law today, the federal courts, using their equity powers, would force the state legislatures to reapportion their congressional districts so as to put an end to anti-urban gerrymandering, that is, would force them to comply with federal law.[16] This lack of federal law, however, is not fortuitous, for the 1929 bill as it was introduced did contain the provision; it was lost through an amendment introduced by men who knew what they were doing.[17] When we consider the fact that additional representatives from the big cities would more than likely be Democrats and that every northern Democrat supported the Housing Act of 1958, for example (and that urban Republicans are more likely than rural Republicans to have supported it), and that the Act had sailed through the Senate, its rejection by the House, by six votes short of the two-thirds majority required to pass it under suspension of the Rules (a device resorted to because of the refusal of the Rules Committee to grant it a rule), can fairly

[15] 37 Stat. 13, Sec. 3.
[16] *Wood* v. *Broom*, 287 U.S. 1 (1932); *Colegrove* v. *Green*, 328 U.S. 549 (1946). Since this was written the Supreme Court has indeed acted, even though Congress has not put back the statutory requirement. In *Baker* v. *Carr*, 82 S. Ct. 691 (1962), the Court held that state apportionment laws are subject to federal judicial review. More precisely, the Court held that a complaint alleging that a state law apportioning *state* legislative seats among the several districts and counties deprives complainants of the equal protection of the laws presents a justiciable cause of action. We can expect the Court to extend this ruling to state laws drawing up congressional districts. Thus, state apportionment laws are now subject to the constitutional requirement of equal protection.
[17] *Congressional Record*, LXIX, 4054; LXX, 1496, 1499, 1584, 1602, 1604; LXXI, 254, 2279, 2280, 2363, 2364, 2444, 2445, 2450.

be attributed to underrepresentation of urban voters in the House of Representatives.[18] This kind of result may fairly be said to have been "planned" in 1929.

There is no intention here to deny that reforms have unforeseen consequences, or that innovations, such as national nominating conventions, introduced for one purpose (in this case to strengthen President Jackson's control over the Democratic party and specifically to ensure the nomination of Martin Van Buren for Vice President) can, especially with the passage of time, serve purposes the opposite of those intended. As William Morris put it: ". . . men fight and lose the battle, and the thing they fought for comes about in spite of their defeat, and when it comes turns out not to be what they meant, and other men have to fight for what they meant under another name."[19] But the truth is that our system of government is a product of both planning and unforeseen adaptation, and to admit the importance of the latter is not to assert the impotence of planning and foresight.

Consider an example of an innovation that has had, and continues to have, tremendous consequences for American politics: the abolition of Negro slavery. This nation willed the abolition of slavery, but surely the antislavery men, including the many zealous and doctrinaire Abolitionists, did not will many of the consequences that followed it. They might not have foreseen them. One man, however, did foresee them, and it is one of the major ironies of history that the man known to the world as the Great Emancipator was extremely reluctant to issue the proclamation from which he derived this title. Anyone who doubts the ability of a man wise in the ways of other men to foresee the consequences of human action, should read Lincoln's message to Congress of December 1, 1862, in which he presented his plan for compensated emancipation and, in the process of

[18] *Congressional Quarterly Almanac*, XIV (1958), 408–9. The original legislation, the National Housing Act of 1949, was enacted in the House by a vote of 227–186, with the Democrats contributing 192 of the majority votes. Of the 55 Democrats who voted against the bill, 52 came from the South or border states. (Arizona, Indiana, and Idaho supplied the other three votes.) *Congressional Quarterly Almanac*, V (1949), 328–29.

[19] *The Dream of John Ball*, in *The Collected Works of William Morris* (London: Longmans, 1912), XVI, 231–32.

defending it, spoke of the probable consequences of the measures that were, unhappily, adopted in its place.

Other examples abound. If it is doubtful that the enfranchisement of women has elevated the moral tone of our politics, the abolition of the two-thirds rule in the Democratic national conventions has certainly reduced the power of the South to influence the choice of the party's candidates for President. If the introduction of "direct democracy" in the form of initiative and referendum did not reduce the power of party bosses, the Seventeenth Amendment certainly did change the character of the Senate in the way it was meant to change it. If the Eighteenth Amendment did not prevent the "manufacture, sale, or transportation of intoxicating liquors" in this country, the Sixteenth Amendment has certainly effected the expected redistribution of wealth that allows the (relatively) richer as well as the (relatively) poorer to consume significant quantities of expensive beverages.

None of this proves, or is meant to prove, either the necessity of party reform or the desirability of any specific reform proposal. It was necessary to belabor what seems an obvious point in order to overcome the "metaphysical" argument that intelligent reform, indeed, intelligence itself, has no role to play in American politics or, specifically, in the shaping of the American system of government.

### III

Except for the proposed constitutional amendments (which could be shown to be less important than some of the other, seemingly more moderate proposals) and some others, the changes proposed by party reformers could be effected by simple majority action in both houses of Congress. (I ignore the possibility of a presidential veto.) The despised seniority system could be replaced whenever a majority in each house agreed to replace it. Senatorial courtesy, according to which the senior senator of a state has a veto power over federal appointments in that state, could be abolished without any formal action whatever. Party finances could probably be centralized and democratized, by which I mean, made to consist of small contributions from many people rather than of large contributions from a few people, by a simple amendment to the Internal Revenue Code, according to which the national committee of each party would be permitted to sell small denominational stamps, not to exceed a maximum of $10, to its members, who would then be permitted to affix these to their tax returns and thereby reduce the amount of their personal income taxes in the amount of the stamp. But there seems little or no desire on the part of Congress to do these things, which makes one suspect that Congress may not be the agency for effecting change in the party system; that on the contrary, because its rules are better adapted to prevention than they are to performance (for example, a motion to table a bill is not debatable, but a motion to consider or reconsider a bill is subject to debate and plenty of it in the Senate), it might be the citadel of power of those most opposed to change. We remember, among other events, that the congressional caucus system for choosing presidential candidates was not replaced by the party convention system because congressmen wanted to be relieved of this great responsibility.

Still, parties and the party system do change. Despite the long history of their names, and despite their habitual invocation of heroic figures from their pasts, neither great party has remained the same party throughout its history. Each has undergone significant changes.

The Jeffersonian republican party, from which the Democratic party is derived, was formed to save the republic from monarchism. Jackson reformed the party by making it a party of the people in order to save the republic from oligarchy. Later it became the party of the slavery interest, and, after slavery, had difficulty being anything until 1932. (A party that nominates Bryan, Parker, Bryan, Wilson, Cox, Davis, and Smith in succession is certainly not agreed on what it is.)

The Republican party came into being to save the country from slavery. During the period of its supremacy after the Civil War it had, as Professor Schattschneider has said,[20] no important positive program of legislation aside from the protective tariff and the gold standard; its purpose, and for this it was admirably

[20] "United States: The Functional Approach to Party Government," in Sigmund Neumann (ed.), *Modern Political Parties: Approaches to Comparative Politics* (Chicago: University of Chicago Press, 1956), p. 197.

organized, was to prevent government action. Efforts were made, notably by Theodore Roosevelt and the elder La Follette, to change it, but these efforts proved unavailing, so that the party today, whether in or out of power, remains a party of opposition, or at most, of not so much or so fast. *The Republican party does not have to be reformed into a strong, centralized, cohesive party to perform this role.*

Changes have indeed been made in both major parties, but these changes have come during periods of crisis and have been effected by an agency outside the Congress, connected somehow with the presidency, or perhaps with the people acting through the presidency. Our history reveals one other important fact about the genesis of these changes: parties have been changed *one at a time*, because some *political* movement or interest used one party to accomplish its purposes. To believe in the possibility of changes in both parties simultaneously is to indulge in illusions. Consider the latest example of a planned change in an American party, that brought about by Franklin Roosevelt and the New Deal, which more than one writer has called the Roosevelt Revolution. It came by means of the Democratic party, not "because the Democratic party was an ideal vehicle for a revolution but because it was the only political instrument available,"[21] to quote Professor Schattschneider, and it came during a period of grave national crisis.

The new Democratic party was organized to save the country again, this time from the "malefactors of great wealth," the "self-seekers" who had betrayed the people's trust, the "money changers [who stood] indicted in the court of public opinion, rejected by the hearts and minds of men" and who had "fled from their high seats in the temple of our civilization." It was the time (and the job of the Democratic party, which had its own share of money changers) to "restore that temple to the ancient truths." How was this program to be accomplished?

> Action in this image and to this end is feasible under the form of government which we have inherited from our ancestors. Our Constitution is so simple and practical that it is possible always to meet extraordinary

[21] *Ibid.*, p. 206.

needs by changes in emphasis and arrangement without loss of essential form. That is why our constitutional system has proved itself the most superbly enduring political mechanism the modern world has produced. It has met every stress of vast expansion of territory, of foreign wars, of bitter internal strife, of world relations. It is to be hoped that the normal balance of executive and legislative authority may be wholly adequate to meet the unprecedented task before us. But it may be that an unprecedented demand and need for undelayed action may call for temporary departure from that normal balance of public procedure.

I am prepared under my constitutional duty to recommend the measures that a stricken Nation in the midst of a stricken world may require. These measures, or such other measures as the Congress may build out of its experience and wisdom, I shall seek, within my constitutional authority, to bring to speedy adoption.

But in the event that the Congress shall fail to take one of these two courses, and in the event that the national emergency is still critical, I shall not evade the clear course of duty that will then confront me. I shall ask the Congress for the one remaining instrument to meet the crisis—broad Executive power to wage a war against the emergency, as great as the power that would be given to me if we were in fact invaded by a foreign foe.

These paragraphs are, of course, from Roosevelt's First Inaugural Address.[22]

So perilous were the times that even Alfred M. Landon, who three-and-a-half years later was to be the Republican candidate to replace Roosevelt, said that "the hand of a national dictator" was preferable to a "paralytic stroke," and offered his assistance "for the duration of the war."[23] Under such circumstances, and with a man of Roosevelt's mind and force of character at the head of the party, capable, as even his enemies will concede, of using the powers of persuasion so effectively, as well as the powers of an extensive federal patronage, it was impossible for

[22] *The Public Papers and Addresses of Franklin D. Roosevelt* (New York: Random House, 1938), II (*The Year of Crisis, 1933*), 14–15. Copyright 1938 by Random House, Inc.

[23] Quoted in Arthur M. Schlesinger, Jr., *The Age of Roosevelt: The Coming of the New Deal* (Boston: Houghton Mifflin, 1959), p. 3.

the Democratic party not to undergo some change. It became, and to some extent still remains, the party that initiates major legislative programs, unprecedented in scope and effect, founded not with a view to the interest of a section or a combination of sections—it has ceased to be mainly a sectional party—but to the alleged welfare of a large class of the people everywhere. With the exception of all of its southern members on one issue and some of its southern members on other issues, it is a party capable of uniting behind a host of major national legislative policies. Whatever has happened to the Republican party since 1932 is the result of the changes wrought in the Democratic party by Franklin Roosevelt, changes inspired and carried out not in order to make the party system more "democratic," but in order to do what he and others believed had to be done to save the nation.

The great changes in our party system have occurred at infrequent intervals, during times of crisis or, at least, alleged crisis, and were initiated or carried through by men—Thomas Jefferson, Andrew Jackson, Abraham Lincoln, and Franklin Roosevelt—who sought and won the presidency. They provided the will, the impetus, the skill, and, by no means insignificantly, great constitutional authority. To state the matter succinctly, our history suggests that changes in the party system can be made only by a President wielding the great power of his office in the name of an aroused people.

## IV

None of this proves that the changes effected by Jefferson, Jackson, Lincoln, and Roosevelt were desirable. A price was paid for each. Indeed, it might be argued that the example of the formation of the Republican party, a party organized along the lines of a sectional opinion, demonstrates the terrible price to be paid for a planned change in the party system, for its first electoral success was followed by the Civil War. While some historians have called the war an irrepressible conflict, others have insisted that it was a repressible, that is, an unnecessary conflict, one that might have been avoided if the political problems that were allowed to sunder the nation had been dealt with instead in the spirit of traditional American compromise. No one was more uncompromising on the basic issue than the presidential candidate chosen by the new Republican party in 1860.

But to concede even so heavy a price does not require us to accept, without argument, the conclusion that the actions of Lincoln and the Republican party were unjustified. To do nothing is easier than to do something; to be governed by events is easier than to attempt to govern them. Specifically, to have accepted a slave code for the territories and to have acquiesced in the Kansas-Nebraska and the Dred Scott decisions would almost certainly have avoided the consequences of the refusal to accept them. Nevertheless, a powerful argument can be made to the effect that the damage inflicted on the country by the Civil War and its aftermath was less than would have been inflicted in the absence of a party leader devoted to the cause of preventing the extension of slavery, even in principle, and willing to use the Republican party as an instrument to prevent its extension. This example from our history shows that the question of change in an established political system must be considered in the light of *all* the foreseeable consequences—not only the consequences of change, but also the consequences of the failure to change. There is no reason to believe, prior to an investigation of the political situation, that the probable consequences of the one will be any more undesirable than the probable consequences of the other.

The political situation today is governed by the grave threat posed by foreign communists. The problems produced by this threat are manifold and urgent. Other problems, not directly related to the dangerous international situation, are less urgent but only relatively less important. It is sufficient to mention racial relations and the congeries of problems associated with our large metropolitan areas. Is our political system now organized to deal effectively with these problems? To use Churchill's test, does it permit decisions in great matters to be taken on their merits, with regard not to a variety of private interests but to the public interest?[24]

The system, designed primarily with a view to limiting government, disperses power among a number of offices, or men

[24] *The World Crisis: The Aftermath* (London: Butterworth, 1929), p. 302.

—the President, administrators, committee chairmen, floor leaders, judges, bosses, patriarchs—but, unfortunately, this fact alone does not provide an answer to the decisive question, whatever the advocates of party reform might contend. Power is certainly dispersed among a number of men, but each of them claims to be acting to advance the public interest, and there is no good reason to conclude, prior to investigation, that even the powerful committee chairman who owes his position to the fact that he has not faced serious electoral competition in thirty years might not be right. Indeed, it could be argued, and not without an element of truth, that the certainty of re-election is highly compatible with the public interest, because it provides the freedom to act on the basis of informed judgment. This was true of Burke. The fact that he sometimes sat for a pocket borough within the gift of Lord Rockingham did not prevent him from being right on many questions—for example, the question of the British response to the revolting American colonies.[25] Dispersion of power does not in itself prevent the public interest from being advanced; it merely makes "responsible" party government difficult to obtain.

Nor would the concentration of power in the hands of a strong centralized party—which means in the hands of the head of the party, the President in our case—guarantee the advancement of the public interest. Britain may be governed by responsible parties, but these party governments are not immune to error, and sometimes on a colossal scale (it is sufficient to recall the pre-World War II Baldwin government). No institutional reform can guarantee the advancement of the public interest. No institutional arrangement will ensure that those who are given power will be able to use that power only when they are right and will be prevented from using it when they are wrong. Yet, in a very real sense, this is what the advocates of party government want: an institutional substitute for practical wisdom. Such a thing does not exist.

This is not to assert with Alexander Pope that only fools contest for forms of government. The substance of policy is of course affected by formal institutions, but whether the institu-

[25] See his speech, "Conciliation with the Colonies," in Hoffman and Levack, *op. cit.*, pp. 61–94.

tions should be changed requires first an examination of the substance of our policy on the great political issues, not an examination of the extent of responsibility, on the mistaken assumption that responsibility and the public interest are the same thing. If our policy has been inadequate, and if its inadequacy can fairly be attributed to institutions, a case is then made for changing the institutions—provided, of course, the probable consequences of the change will be preferable to the probable consequences of the failure to change.

A case is frequently made for changes that will enable the federal government to act with greater vigor in the areas of both foreign and domestic policy. Especially with respect to the international situation, a severely limited government is a luxury the country can no longer afford. But does vigorous and comprehensive executive action in the United States, which is what vigorous government amounts to, depend on changing the system? To be specific (and to put an end to the illusion that the question of changes in the party system can be discussed without involvement in partisan disputes), was the lack of a strong conventional military force attributable to the lack of executive power? Or must it not be attributed to former President Eisenhower's conviction that a force on the order of that proposed by some military men, and by others, was not only unnecessary but too expensive? (The American taxpayer, he said on one occasion, was one of the greatest casualties of the cold war.) Can the failure to deal adequately with the problem of river pollution be attributed to the lack of executive power? Or must it not be attributed in part to President Eisenhower's belief that no problem is more local than river pollution (a statement that will be contested by those who live downstream on an interstate river)? Can the lack of a larger urban renewal program be attributed to the lack of executive power? Or is not President Eisenhower's 1959 veto partly responsible? To these examples others might be added. The fact is, for eight years not much was attempted, which means that there has been no demonstration in our time that Franklin Roosevelt was wrong when he said in his First Inaugural Address: "Our Constitution is so simple and practical that it is possible always to meet extraordinary needs by changes in emphasis and arrangement without loss of essential form."[26] Whatever the amount of disagreement on these political issues, there is likely to be agreement that President Eisenhower did not regard the system to be inadequate for the tasks at hand, as he saw them.

President Kennedy may come to the conclusion that changes are needed, but this surely will be the result only of a failure to obtain the consent of Congress to policies and programs that he deems essential to the well-being of the country. Only after his policy proposals have been rejected (or he has been convinced, as Lincoln was in the case of his plan for compensated emancipation, that it would be useless to try to gain that consent), will he or should he make an effort to change the system. Nothing has yet occurred to justify the risk of alienating members of both parties in Congress, as reform proposals are likely to do, and at this writing he has not exhausted the means available to him of obtaining that consent: for example, an appeal to the people in order to overcome the opposition of a recalcitrant Congress.

Let us presume that such an appeal becomes necessary in order to enact some major defense legislation (perhaps a civil defense program), and as a result of this appeal he acquires the support of a majority in the House and Senate. Is it possible to believe on the basis of our experience that the will of this majority, backed by the President and the people, will be frustrated by a committee chairman, or by the rules of either house? It is contended here that this is extremely unlikely—except in one area of public policy, race relations. One authority on American politics says bluntly that when "such a majority exists, it gets what it wants."[27] But this means, except for this one area, that the power needed to effect a change in the system will make the change unnecessary, for the power needed to change will suffice to get the substantive policy adopted!

Certainly it would be simpler for the President to obtain the consent of Congress were he the head of a united party that enjoys a majority in both houses. But is it a matter of concern to the nation—as opposed to the devotees of a particular theory

[26] Whether the changes in the reading of the Constitution by the Supreme Court, which were a necessary condition of much of the New Deal, were changes in emphasis and arrangement or in essential form, need not be discussed here.

[27] Rossiter, *op. cit.*, p. 64.

of democracy—whether that consent comes wholly or predominantly from his own party or from a coalition from both parties? It ought not to be; what ought to matter is the policy adopted. The Constitution requires the President to govern and the Congress to give or withhold consent, but we rely primarily on the President to supply the practical wisdom needed to govern well. If he is stupid or vicious, we rely—perhaps in vain—on the ability of Congress to check his stupidity and viciousness. This is done more readily if members of Congress retain a measure of independence from the Executive greater than that enjoyed by the backbenchers of the strongly centralized parties in the British House of Commons. If, on the other hand, the people were to ignore the President's appeal for a reasonable program, and this congressional independence were used to thwart its adoption, it would not be the parties that need to be reformed; it would be the American people.

It is conceded that to rely on the President to this extent is to "virtually insure a government by fits and starts," as Stephen Bailey says,[28] but there seems to be no alternative to this, short of abolishing the presidency as we know it. The office is much too powerful not to play the decisive role in our system of government, which means that the character of our government is largely determined by the character of the man who is President. Congress cannot govern; the national conventions cannot govern. As for party councils, the establishment of which was heralded by party reformers,[29] the Democratic Advisory Council was abolished within a few weeks of Kennedy's taking office, and there is no reason to doubt that a similar fate awaits an equivalent Republican body under similar circumstances.

In summary, there is good reason to believe that the power needed to govern the United States effectively is available to the President who asks for it, and if it should turn out that it is not available, the fault lies not with the party system but with the American people themselves.

[28] Bailey, p. 3.
[29] *Ibid.*, p. 7.

# HARRY V. JAFFA

•

# THE NATURE AND ORIGIN
# OF THE AMERICAN PARTY SYSTEM

There is general agreement that political parties are necessary for the functioning of what we today call free government. At one end of the spectrum of opinion, Professor Berns somewhat reservedly says that the role assigned to parties in our system is "indispensable." Professor Banfield, at the other extreme, appears to assign many if not all good results of the American political system to the party system. Indeed, at times he seems to regard the party system as the fundamental political phenomenon, the heart of the polity considered as an organic whole. "It has provided governments which . . . have been humane and, in some crises, bold and enterprising; . . . it has tended to check violence, moderate conflict, and narrow the cleavages within the society. . . . Not only has the American party system produced good results, it has produced better ones than have been produced almost anywhere else by other systems." To hold such language about the Constitution or, as Berns does, about American political heroes, usually presidents, is familiar. To hold it with regard to the parties which, like Congress, are usually objects of deprecation in American folklore, is both bold and unusual. It is quite consistent, moreover, with Banfield's thesis that "A political system is an accident." One can, I think, consider the American political system as essentially unplanned, if one considers that the party system is the central or prime feature of the whole. For the party system, or political parties as we now know them, were certainly no ingredient in the government envisaged by the Founding Fathers. What *they* called parties had only an equivocal connection with what we call

59

parties, and the parties they observed (although expecting them always to exist) they regarded as, at best, necessary evils. That something called political parties should one day receive the encomiums lavished upon American parties by Banfield would have seemed incredible to them, and is assuredly a profound irony. How did this come about? What can justify it? I am not certain I can answer the latter question, although I shall try. To the former I can at least offer hypotheses in which I have some confidence.

## I

Banfield has defended the American party system. Berns has taken the view that most of the benefits attributed to it by Banfield are due to other causes, or to a concatenation of causes in which the role of parties has been secondary. I should like, first of all, to offer some theoretical formulations of the functions which, it is generally admitted, ought to be performed by political parties in our form of government. Banfield, it is true, seems to deny that theory has any proper place in the assignment of functions to parties. Nevertheless, I believe that a theory does underlie his view; or, at the least, that a theoretical justification of the role of political parties can be offered for his view.

What is a political party? Broadly speaking, I would distinguish two answers to this question current today. Both, of course, are addressed to the problem of governing in accordance with the principles of democracy in a mass, heterogeneous society. Both understand that government in such a society requires a foundation of active consent by the governed. And the political society is conceived as supplying that systematized communication of governors and governed which is productive of such consent. The mere legal machinery of representative government is recognized on all sides to be insufficient. The voters must be drawn into the process of nominating candidates and formulating policies. This process must be more or less continuous, and requires a continuing institution—the party. From these general points of agreement, however, we can now specify some grounds of divergence.

According to one view, it is essential to a democracy that the voters be confronted with a genuine choice of alternative candidates and alternative policies. It is only in virtue of alternatives, it is held, that government can remain responsive to the will, opinion, or consent of the governed. One-party government is a mockery of democracy, but tweedledum and tweedledee are one-party government in disguise. The function of the majority party is to organize and administer the government; the function of the minority, to criticize the performance of the majority, to confront the electorate with alternative personnel and policies, to stand ready to assume the responsibilities of governing.

Others, however, see the function of party differently. Parties, they say, do not and cannot—except in comparatively rare and extreme situations—stand for genuine alternatives. This, it is held, follows from the genuine and desirable diversity within a democratic society. A democratic government stands or falls pre-eminently upon its ability to do two things: to represent a majority, and to protect the indefeasible rights of minorities. But a majority can arise only if a broadly based consensus is created out of the infinitely varied, contrary, and sometimes contradictory demands of the electorate. Yet this consensus *must* be created, if we are not to have minority government, or coalition government, which is perforce without moral weight, and is weak and ineffectual. The political party must then find a common denominator in the demands of groups numerous enough to comprise a majority of the country. According to this second viewpoint, the party is primarily the instrument of consensus, rather than the instrument of choice.

This second, or consensus theory, to repeat, takes as its fundamental fact the diversity which exists in a true democracy. "Liberty is to faction what air is to fire," wrote Madison in the famous tenth *Federalist,* and for this reason, he held, "it is *civilized* nations," i.e., free nations, that are divided into "a landed interest, a manufacturing interest, a mercantile interest, a moneyed interest, [and] many lesser interests."[1] Freedom of political choice manifests itself, accordingly, not in sharply contrasting major alternatives, but in the facility—not to say promiscuity—with which the multifarious groups and interests peddle their votes and influence. It is because a democratic government has no will independent of society, *and* because there

[1] Ed. Edward Mead Earle (New York: Modern Library, 1941) , p. 55.

is no monolithic majority that can afford to be indifferent to minorities, that we have political freedom. Even the largest minority in a free society cannot hope to govern without the support of many interests different from its own pre-eminent interest. For this reason the democratic political process involves a continuing search for a majority, which is a search for consensus—and this search is the condition which ensures a concern for the interests and rights of minorities.

Further: party platforms, and government policies, cannot reflect consensus if the grounds of difference among competing political demands are not obscured, rather than clarified. It is, therefore, both inevitable, and desirable, that major parties, in the pursuit of majority status, should tend to resemble each other. The reason for this can be expressed almost in mathematical form: if a minority deserts a major party, it subtracts from it a certain number of votes—a number which may spell the difference between victory and defeat. Since elections are frequently close in the United States (as in most free countries), the influence of any given minority may be much greater than its size would indicate. But this influence will correspond to a double numerical value if the minority in question can not only desert one major party, but can join itself to another. The psychological propensities accompanying this "formula" are twofold: on the one hand, it means that each major party is under an inducement to be hospitable to minorities within the opposing party; and, on the other, that minorities are under an inducement so to moderate their demands that they are negotiable with *both* the major parties. Hence we see that a very intense competition between major parties arises, and can arise, from their similarity, rather than from their dissimilarity; and that the condition which favors competition between parties, also favors that moderation in political demands which makes majority rule feasible.

From the foregoing it will appear that, according to the consensus theory, fundamental political decisions are frequently made, and should be made, in the process whereby groups negotiate within parties, rather than in the decisions at the polls. For example, the choice of Willkie over Taft, Dewey over Taft, and Eisenhower over Taft, by Republican nominating conventions, may be said to be acts of democratic choice, even if they were more fundamental for the direction of public policy than the choice at the polls of Roosevelt over Willkie and Dewey, or Eisenhower over Stevenson. In both instances there was a judgment of the Republican delegates that the ground of majority consensus lay in what came to be called Modern Republicanism. This judgment reveals a flaw—as it seems to me—in the consensus theory. For the continuing conviction, since 1936, of where the ground of consensus in American politics lies, was the result of the 1936 election, in which the voters *were* presented with a fairly downright choice between Old Republicanism and New Dealism. It was the Republican catastrophe of that year which seems to have convinced most delegates to subsequent conventions of the party that that particular set of alternatives, or anything closely resembling it, should never again be presented to the voters. What seems to happen, then, is that at a very few, and very widely spaced elections, the voters are faced with drastically different alternatives. The function of these elections is not, however, to preserve freedom of choice, in any doctrinal sense. For the result of such elections is to virtually annihilate one of the alternatives, and to reveal the new ground upon which consensus must be sought by *both* parties in the next generation.

I think we may conclude that the alternatives theory, and the consensus theory, are both true in a sense—they are true abstractions concerning how the party system functions (and how it *ought* to function) at *different* times. Once a party has demonstrated a winning formula in American politics, then the opposition, to survive, must recast itself—at least to a considerable extent—in the image of its victorious rival. This remains the case until radically different conditions and different issues arise —conditions and issues which portend a drastic realignment of the entire bipolar arrangement. Some time during this process of realignment, and then only, is there apt to be an election in which the parties stand for radically different things.

II

An adequate theoretical approach to American political parties, I believe, would have to account for, and justify, in a unified explanation, the phenomena separately accounted for and justified by the alternatives and the consensus theories. Banfield's approach places him squarely within the framework of the consensus theory, a theory which is indeed sufficient for most of our politics most of the time. But the few occasions upon which our parties stood for genuine and profound alternatives, alternatives profoundly ideological, and having to do with the very basis of society, have been supremely significant for everything that has come after them. If our parties had not sometimes stood for alternatives in a sense that Banfield appears to deplore, they could not have created consensus in the intervening years. In particular I should like to note that in Banfield's view, "except for the Civil War" our party system "has tended to check violence, moderate conflict, and narrow the cleavages within the society." While it is true that, happily, we have not had more than one Civil War, I believe that the Civil War, even if an exception in one sense, is also the most characteristic phenomenon in American politics, if by characteristic we mean that which reveals the innermost character of that politics. During the administrations of James Monroe, party feeling in this country became nearly extinct. "The election of 1820 was not even a contest. . . . Mr. Monroe was elected by a vote which would have been absolutely unanimous had not one elector of New Hampshire, deeming it due to the memory of Washington that no President after him should share in the honor of a unanimous election, given his vote for John Quincy Adams."[2]

There was, however, one profound political struggle during Monroe's administration; that was the struggle culminating in the Missouri Compromise. It was not, however, a party struggle. But the political lines drawn in that struggle corresponded closely with the party lines in 1860. In my view, the political parties of the generation after 1820, were really called into existence by the issues of the Civil War, and the Civil War was very much the culmination of the party conflict. However, that is to anticipate somewhat too much. Here let me note that John Quincy Adams, Monroe's successor, in 1824 said, "I shall [if elected] exclude no person for political opinions or for personal

[2] Edward Stanwood, *A History of Presidential Elections* (4th ed.; Boston and New York: Houghton, Mifflin, 1892), p. 70.

opposition to me. My great object will be to break up the remnant of old party distinctions and bring the whole people together in sentiment as much as possible."

Adams was elected in the House of Representatives that year, because the division of the electoral vote among Adams, Jackson, Crawford, and Clay kept any one of them from securing a majority, although Jackson's total, 99, was greater than Adams' 84, and was a fair measure of his superiority in the popular vote. But all the candidates were Republicans, and their rivalry was for the most part personal. Adams' idea of removing the last vestiges of party distinction is obviously reminiscent of Jefferson's "we are all republicans—we are all federalists." But there is the grimmest irony in the sequel. As Henry Adams has shown, what Jefferson meant by "we are all republicans—we are all federalists" was that there was room for only one political party in the country. Jefferson thus proceeded to cajole, coax, and suborn part of the federalist party (John Quincy Adams being the most famous of the converts) to republicanism, while placing the remainder on the road to ultimate political extinction. Jefferson, who played the role of party leader to the hilt, succeeded, as we have observed, in virtually ending party distinctions (for Monroe was in this respect merely the executor of Jefferson's political legacy). Adams, who sincerely abjured the party role, paved the way for the revival of parties, and for an ascendancy of party feeling that culminated, and in my view, could only culminate, in the Civil War.

The original Jacksonian issue was the allegedly "stolen" election of 1824, when a "deal" between Adams and Clay deprived the popular candidate of the victory which, by popular principles, was rightfully his. This, in itself, was an ideological issue, in that it expressed itself as the cause of democracy against scheming oligarchy, even though the election had been decided in strict accordance with the Constitution. There is particular irony in the fact that it was the absence of party nominating machinery rather than an oligarchic plot, which was the actual sufficient cause of Adams' election in the House of Representatives. But if the first impulse of Jacksonian Democracy came from a transient, and somewhat artificial issue, its second impulse, and its profoundest embodiment, in the war against the

second Bank of the United States, was neither transient nor artificial. It was an ideological issue which raised all the old ghosts
of the classical Jeffersonian revolutionary crusade against "monocratic" federalism. This republicanism culminated in the election
of 1800, as a result of the struggle against the Alien and Sedition
Acts. Republican doctrine was fashioned in the Virginia and
Kentucky Resolutions, expounded by Madison in his Report to
the Virginia Assembly, and elaborated dialectically in the writings by John Taylor of Caroline, and the speeches of John
Randolph, among others. We must presently examine some main
elements of this, the first great party doctrine in American
history.[3]

## III

Before doing so, I should like to consider briefly Banfield's case
against those who prefer "democracy of procedure" to "production of, and maintenance of, a good society." I wholly endorse
the substance of the case he makes against certain theorists, and
I would like to elaborate that case by insisting that their error
lies, not so much in preferring procedure to result, as in having
a false conception of democratic procedure. As Jefferson said in
his first inaugural address, absolute acquiescence in the decision
of the majority is the vital principle of republics. A theory
which, therefore, places paramount stress upon the representation of different opinions, without regard for the consequences
to majority rule, cannot be democratic or republican, in the
Jeffersonian sense. A theorist like Duverger would encourage
tendencies which make majority rule impossible, by so dividing
the citizen body that no majority existed. Of his doctrine, I believe, the same can be said as Lincoln, in his first inaugural address, said of secession:

> Plainly, the central idea of secession, is the essence
> of anarchy. A majority, held in restraint by constitu-
> tional checks and limitations, and always changing
> easily with deliberate changes of popular opinions and

---

[3] In this essay I deliberately pass over the peculiar significance of agrar-
ianism in the fundamentalist republican position, since I have discussed it at
some length in "Agrarian Virtue and Republican Freedom: An Historical
Perspective," in Center for Agricultural and Economic Adjustment, *Goals and
Values in Agricultural Policy* (Ames: Iowa State University Press, 1961).

sentiments is the only true sovereign of a free people. Whoever rejects it, does, of necessity, fly to anarchy or to despotism. Unanimity is impossible; the rule of a minority, as a permanent arrangement, is wholly inadmissible; so that rejecting the majority principle, anarchy or despotism in some form is all that is left.

Since anarchy can continue only for a brief time, despotism is always the probable result either of secession or of that false theoretical democracy which admits to a legitimate role within the body politic such differences of opinion as would prevent majority rule.

If, moreover, the citizens differ among themselves on questions concerning the very basis of society, they cannot, in a moral sense, be fellow-citizens. Without agreement on fundamentals there can be no trust, and without trust there is no basis for citizenship. Free government, properly so called, involves ruling and being ruled in turn. Men cannot confide into the hands of others their families, their property, or their religion, if they think those others are fundamentally hostile or indifferent to them. Majority rule presupposes an agreement, more or less unanimous, on the all-inclusive aims of life, as they may be touched by the action of government. It cannot create such agreement. Duverger's theory presupposes a condition in which the possibility of democratic government may not exist, and instead of considering how such a condition may be transformed, proposes instead to institutionalize it. Let me now recur further to the logical ground of the idea of majority rule, particularly as we have received it from the Declaration of Independence.

The Declaration teaches that, in accordance with the laws of nature and of nature's God, all men are created equal, that they are endowed by their Creator with certain unalienable rights, and that the just powers of government are derived from the consent of the governed. The equality of all men is said to be a self-evident truth. What can possibly be meant by such an assertion? It cannot mean that all men are equal in intelligence, strength, beauty, or in moral or intellectual capacity. It does mean that there is no natural difference between man and man, such as there is between man and every other species of animal, that makes one man *by nature* the ruler of another man. Any man is by nature the ruler of any dog—even, we must add, if the dog chases him up a tree—as he is by nature the ruler of any monkey—even if the monkey evades him by swinging on the branches of a tree. One man may rule another by force or by fraud, but such rule is not natural, as is the rule of man over other species. As a result of accident or misfortune—but not nature—a man may, like a child, require to be ruled by another for his own good. But no mature normal human being is by nature the subject of any other human being, and rule which is not natural may be *legitimate* if, and only if, there is authority conferred by agreement or *consent*.

What kind of agreement gives rise to legitimate authority? Certainly not every kind. The Declaration says that men have unalienable rights. There can be no legitimate exercise of political power in violation of those rights, however much men may be duped or defrauded into agreeing to it. "But our rulers," wrote Jefferson, in the *Notes on Virginia,* "can have no authority over such natural rights [e.g., those enumerated in the Declaration], only as we have submitted to them. The rights of conscience we never submitted, we could not submit. We are answerable for them to our God. The legitimate powers of government extend to such acts only as are injurious to others. But it does me no injury for my neighbor to say there are twenty Gods, or no God. It neither picks my pocket or breaks my leg." Here is a crucial consideration: on the premises of the Declaration, only men who have a knowledge of natural right, and of the difference between the just and unjust powers of government, can give that enlightened form of consent which alone gives rise to legitimate government. "An *elective despotism* was not the government we fought for," Jefferson also wrote in the *Notes.* The form of government, and majority rule itself, is no guarantee against despotism, if the principles animating those forming the government are not the principles of free men. Consent alone can confer legitimacy upon the powers of government, but consent is only a necessary, not a sufficient, condition. *Enlightened* consent is the necessary *and* sufficient condition.

What constitutes enlightenment, according to the ancestral faith of Americans? Consider the doctrine of the equality of all men in its relation to the evil teachings of National Socialism and of Communism. Because of the theory of racial inequality, the Nazis held that inferior races could be used as means to the ends of the master-race with no more restraint than we practice in the use of cattle. Indeed, they practiced a good deal less than that, since most of us believe that not even cattle should be subject to more pain than is unavoidable, as we process them for their meat and hides. The lampshades of human parchment are symbolic of the Nazi denial of the relevance of the difference between the species for moral and political right. If the Nazis were not (and I do not know that they were not) cannibals, it is only because they had not acquired a taste for human flesh. National Socialism is a by-product, however corrupt and perverted, of the evolutionary hypothesis. According to this hypothesis, the differences of the species are not fixed and unalterable, but are only well-marked and widely separated varieties. More fundamental, the existence of what we call species does not reflect any moral purpose in the universe, but only the chance or necessity governing biological causation. The very idea of "laws of Nature and of Nature's God" ceases to have moral meaning. The difference between man and monkey is a difference of degree, not of kind. Hence the potential if not actual difference between one variety or race of mankind (e.g., the Nordic race) and other varieties (e.g., Negroes and Jews) may be as great as between what we call man and what we call simian. From the point of view of the Nazi, the destruction of millions of Jews and others of allegedly inferior races was no less justified than our destruction of millions of monkeys in the manufacture of polio vaccine. Indeed, to them the virus of racial contagion was the more sinister.

The moral essence of Marxism and of Nazism are the same. In the one case there is a master-race, in the other a master-class. The party-structure and leadership which claim to embody the consciousness and directing intelligence of the race of the future or the class of the future, lay claim to a moral right and superiority in relation to other men which, in the Declaration of Independence, may be enjoyed only by men in their relations with other species, but never by man in relation to man. Both Nazism and Communism present themselves as versions of the hypothesis that says that higher forms are created out of the struggle of lower forms of life, by a law which guarantees the victory of the superior, and simultaneously justifies it in its subjection or destruction of all antagonistic forms. From this it will, I hope, appear that the doctrine in the Declaration of Independence of the self-evidence of the difference between man and other species, and its absolute moral significance, is *the* premise of the laws of Nature and of Nature's God. This premise, it is true, has been gravely questioned by scientific developments since the eighteenth century. However the course of science can, as it must, raise theoretical doubts concerning this and every other premise of human thought, it remains the necessary moral and political premise of everything we call humane and decent. And it describes rather precisely, I think, why neither Nazis or Communists can be either required, or permitted, to form an element in that opinion whose consent supplies the ground of legitimate government. At the same time, it indicates why the proportional representation of opinion, as such, ought not, and cannot, be the ground of democratic procedure. Only those opinions in which the moral ingredient of the laws of Nature and of Nature's God is given due weight can have a role in creating legitimate government.

## IV

To understand the nature of American politics, and therewith of American party politics, one must, I believe, recognize the derivation of certain ideological problems from the Declaration of Independence itself. Notwithstanding the differences between the American, French, and Russian revolutions, there are parallels whose significance cannot be disregarded. Indeed, only a careful understanding of similarities will enable us to preserve the differences. By the teaching of the Declaration, the consent of the governed means the consent of the *enlightened*. Those who do not have the necessary minimum knowledge of human nature cannot recognize its rights, and those who do not recognize the rights of others, cannot be entrusted with their government. Free government is not possible among men who believe that some are born permanently to rule, and others merely to be ruled. "America was the only spot in the political world where the principles of universal reformation could begin," wrote Tom Paine in *The Rights of Man*. The primary reason for this was that it was the only place where the popular superstitions which entrusted authority to priests and kings were sufficiently attenuated to enable popular government to strike roots. From America, Paine believed, popular enlightenment would flow back to the Old World. Concerning the election which produced the States-General, from which the French Revolution in 1789 took its beginning, he wrote:

> The election which followed was not a contested election, but an animated one. The candidates were not men, but principles. Societies were formed in Paris, and committees of correspondence and communication established throughout the Nation, for the purpose of enlightening the people, and explaining to them the principles of civil government. . . .[4]

The committees of which Paine speaks were, in his view, the French equivalents of the American committees which had led to the resistance to the Stamp Act, then to the Continental Congress, and finally to independence. In France, of course, it led to the Jacobin clubs. These clubs, or their leaders, being possessed of "the principles of civil government" in the midst of unenlightened masses whose interests they alone grasped, eventually felt compelled to use, and justified in using, extremely authoritarian means in admitting and excluding from a share of civil government. However much we may deplore the eventual degeneration of the Jacobins, particularly in the Reign of Terror under the Committee of Public Safety, we must recognize that to many contemporaries the Jacobins were merely following the example—under much less favorable circumstances—of the American revolutionary committees, which had dealt rough justice (and injustice) to American Tories. Still more important, we must recognize that the first American political party, properly so-called, the Jeffersonian Republican party, was an outgrowth of democratic societies that had sprung up here during Washington's administration. These were partly stimulated by the French Revolution, but in the main were the result of a con-

[4] (Everyman's Lib.; New York: Dutton, 1951), p. 87.

viction that Federalist policies would undo the work of the American Revolution, and lead us back into the fold of Britain and of monarchy.

The word "party" in the eighteenth century derived its primary meaning from its association with partisanship. There were two principal, original causes of partisanship. The most famous we are familiar with from the tenth *Federalist*:

> The latent causes of faction are thus sown in the nature of man; and we see them everywhere brought into different degrees of activity, according to the different circumstances of civil society. A zeal for different opinions concerning religion, concerning government, and many other points, as well of speculation as of practice . . . have . . . divided mankind into parties, inflamed them with mutual animosity, and rendered them much more disposed to vex and oppress each other than to cooperate for their common good. . . . But the most common and durable source of factions has been the various and unequal distribution of property. Those who hold and those who are without property have ever formed distinct interests in society. Those who are creditors, and those who are debtors, fall under a like discrimination. A landed interest, a manufacturing interest, a mercantile interest, a moneyed interest, with many lesser interests, grow up of necessity in *civilized* nations, and divide them into different classes, actuated by different sentiments and views. The regulation of these various and interfering interests forms the principal task of *modern* legislation, and involves the spirit of party and faction in the necessary and ordinary operations of the government. [Italics added.][5]

Nature is the primary cause of partisanship. Nature, which is the cause of our rights, also endows us with passions which, in the pursuit of our peculiar attachments, bias our judgment and corrupt our integrity. Yet a *civilized, modern* nation is one in which there is the maximum degree of liberty, and in which nature is, in one sense, given the greatest scope. It is possible, Madison says, to give "every citizen the same opinions, the same passions, and the same interests." This is what the medieval polity substantially attempted, as did the more recent absolute

[5] *Op. cit.,* p. 55.

monarchies which united church and state. This is what modern totalitarian regimes attempt, with far greater means of success, and far greater success. Thus, the second great cause of partisanship is the partisanship of those who would set up and preserve a regime of liberty. Perhaps we should add as a third cause the negative of the second, the cause animating those who oppose the regime of liberty.

To repeat: the primary cause of parties is human nature, conceived as passionate, antisocial egotism. A second cause is that of those animated by a knowledge of human nature, who would set up a regime of liberty, and so dispose the competing interests of an emancipated human nature that they are permitted or compelled to co-operate for the common good. A third cause is that of the reactionary opponents of the regime of liberty, whether American Tories during the Revolution or secret counterrevolutionaries after it (e.g., the Essex Junto). These are the counterparts of the French émigrés who could learn nothing and forget nothing. Of these three causes of parties, producing three kinds of parties, one only can be considered intrinsically good: the cause of the party of the regime of liberty. But the necessity of such a party, and its justification, is only conditional. As Jefferson once observed, if knaves and rogues organize, good men must do so also. At the moment Jefferson had in mind the "monocrats" of Hamilton's persuasion, as Jefferson understood that persuasion. But Jefferson believed such counterrevolutionary forces could be finally eliminated from political life; and John Quincy Adams, as the legatee both of his father and of Jefferson—i. e., of the leaders of both political parties in the bitter election of 1800—believed he would preside over the final liquidation of political parties in America.

But what of the political parties founded upon the natural zeal for different opinions, above all those arising from that most durable cause of difference, the "various and unequal distribution of property"? What Madison calls *parties* we call *interest groups*. What we call parties, and what Banfield rightly praises for ameliorating differences amongst us and making the success of our system possible, is in one sense the direct opposite of what Madison calls parties. The Democratic and Republican parties of today are institutions which, outside the formal, legal structure of government, reduce the number and intensity of struggling factions, so that they are amenable to the public interest and susceptible of being welded into majorities, or minorities capable of becoming majorities. Still, this is not the whole truth. Our conception of political party has one element in common with what Madison calls parties. That element arises from the fact that each of our great parties has always in its inception, and in its moment of greatest victory, identified its opposite as the party opposed to the regime of liberty. Jefferson's party in 1800, Jackson's in 1828 and 1832, Lincoln's in 1860, has regarded the opposition to its cause as that of those "united and actuated by some common impulse of passion, or of interest, adverse to the rights of other citizens, or to the permanent and aggregate interests of the community." American political parties in their greatest moments, in the moments which create the morale upon which the party lives for generations afterwards, appear *to themselves* as great revolutionary uprisings of the proponents of the regime of liberty, to expel from the body politic or, at the least, to render harmless to the body politic, the virus of opinions which are false in relation to the rights of human nature. According to Jefferson monarchical opinions had no right within a republican society, and according to Lincoln the same was true of opinions holding slavery to be a positive good.

The great difficulty in regard to American political parties arises when, after the expulsion of these devils, the party which expelled them has then to reconcile the legitimate, but still pernicious factions arising from merely selfish (but not ideological) self-interest. Or perhaps we should say that it arises from the fact that this more limited, and highly desirable function, must be performed in an atmosphere in which ideological struggle is never wholly absent, and in which the memory of the ideological struggle must always be evoked to provide the morale of the parties. If the ideological struggle had in fact ever withered away, as Jefferson and John Quincy Adams expected, this problem would not have continued to the present day. But if ideological problems had not recurred in American politics, contrary to the founders' expectation, and contrary to what we find pronounced by many present-day political scientists, perhaps political parties *would* have withered away.

# The Nature and Origin of the American Party System

Let us now ask why the founding generation expected the task which we assign to our major political parties, of ameliorating the struggle of factions or interest groups, to be performed either inside or outside the legislature, without the auxiliary aid of such an institution.

I think there were two sets of assumptions, among the men whom we call the founders of our political system, as to how the clashes of interest engendered by human nature, in a regime of liberty, were to be resolved. The first of these is the one we least commonly associate with Madison, because it is farthest from the doctrine of the tenth and fifty-first *Federalist,* wherein we find Madison's most famous theoretical formulations. But it is the doctrine upon which the Jeffersonian republican party was largely based, and which Madison was compelled to give lip-service to, and which involved him in the great and massive contradiction which is the outstanding feature and problem of his career. That doctrine is perhaps most conveniently summed up in Tom Paine's *Rights of Man,* the first part of which was published here in 1791, in the midst of the burgeoning quarrel of Jefferson and Madison with Adams and Hamilton. It was published with a note by Jefferson prominently displayed on the masthead, saying that he was "extremely pleased to find it [*The Rights of Man*] will be re-printed here, and that something is at length to be publicly said against the political heresies which have sprung up among us." Jefferson, be it noted, never hesitated to speak of the evil of political heresy, or to insist that the strength of republican government could be no greater than the purity of the republican doctrine held by the citizenry. The following is from the first chapter of the second part of *The Rights of Man*:

> Great part of that order which reigns among mankind is not the effect of Government. It has its origin in the principles of society and the natural constitution of man. It existed prior to Government, and would exist if the formality of Government was abolished. The mutual dependence and reciprocal interest which man has upon man, and all the great parts of civilised community upon each other, create that great chain of connection which holds it together. The landholder, the farmer, the manufacturer, the merchant, the tradesman,

and every occupation, prospers by the aid which each re-
ceives from the other, and from the whole. Common interest regulates their concerns, and forms their law;
. . . society performs for itself almost everything which
is ascribed to Government. . . .

There is a natural aptness in man, and more so in
society, because it embraces a greater variety of abilities
and resources, to accommodate itself to whatever situation it is in. The instant formal Government is abolished, society begins to act: a general association takes
place, and common interest produces common security. . . .

The more perfect civilization is, the less occasion
has it for Government, because the more it does regulate its own affairs, and govern itself. . . .[6]

Paine is far more extreme in his formulations than is Jefferson,
but his doctrinal boldness is an indispensable gloss upon the
sounding words of Jefferson's first inaugural:

. . . what more is necessary to make us a happy and
prosperous people? Still one thing more, fellow-citizens
—a wise and frugal government, which shall restrain
men from injuring one another, which shall leave them
otherwise free to regulate their own pursuits of industry
and improvement, and shall not take from the mouth
of labor the bread it has earned. This is the sum of
good government. . . .

In Paine and Jefferson we see the idea expressed, that that government is best which governs least. Here also we see the doctrine which, in the history of human thought, precedes and in
some measure anticipates the doctrine that, in the optimum case,
political government shall wither away.

In the original Jeffersonian theory, there is a natural harmony in the selfish interests which create society, and the main
business of national legislation is the negative one of preventing
the foisting upon society of those interests which depend for
their existence upon government. As Jefferson and Paine saw
Great Britain, the main interests of that government arose from
the dynastic interests of the monarchy and of the oligarchy
which fed them and fed upon them. The commercial interests
incorporated in and symbolized by the Bank of England had

[6] *Op. cit.,* pp. 157–59.

prospered by privileges which the monarchy had helped extend. These interests supported in turn the interests of the monarchy by helping the king corrupt parliament. The result was the whole system of monopoly which was the empire, and the dynastic wars which created and enlarged that system. It was all a plot by the few against the many, and a denial of the rights of human nature. A national debt, a national bank, a large central government with many sinecures at its disposal, and in particular a central government with a large military or naval establishment, were evil. Every one of these things separately and all together had the tendency to produce monarchy. To avert monarchy was the duty of all republicans. Here is the original program of Jeffersonian republicanism, the doctrinal basis of the election of 1800, which Jefferson himself called a greater revolution than that of 1776.

The Jeffersonian passion can only be grasped by grasping the significance to the republicans of the 1790's of the revolution in France, and of the reaction to that revolution in Britain and America. Jefferson thought that the Burke of the *Thoughts on the Cause of the Present Discontents* and of the *Conciliation with America* had sold out to the corrupt regime he had previously denounced, and he saw the federalists as trying to produce in America the same corrupt British regime that Burke had once so brilliantly described. Hamilton's funding system, his assumption of state debts, his national bank, his protective tariff proposals, his desire for a standing army, were all seen as a reproduction of the elements of the British court and court policy. Adams' predilection for British pomp and circumstance, capped finally by his signing of the Alien and Sedition Acts, indicated the implacable resolve of a class bent upon privilege and intent upon persecuting out of existence a regime based upon the equal rights of man. Here also we see the fusion of an ideological crusade with a practical program for interest groups capable of forming a majority consensus, which is the characteristic feature of the American party system.

## V

The second great and characteristic assumption among the founding generation we have already seen expressed in the tenth *Federalist*. It holds that the "interfering interests" of a free society must be regulated, because it sees no such natural harmony in society as Paine sees. Or, rather, it sees harmony arising rather from the deliberate arrangement of interests by government, as the integral element in the creation of the common good. It sees no such radical distinction as Paine describes, setting Society apart from Government.

According to the tenth *Federalist,* the central government in the large republic created by the new Constitution would have both a greater ability and a greater inclination to govern for the common good than would more narrowly circumscribed governments. The reasons for these expectations are familiar. The first is that, by extending the sphere encompassing parties and interests, as one does in the extensive republic envisaged by the Constitution, one makes it more difficult for a majority to be formed which is dominated by a single interest or passion, a majority which would ride roughshod over the interests of others. The second reason is that the operation of the elective principle, in this greater republic, is more likely to produce "representatives whose enlightened views and virtuous sentiments render them superior to local prejudices and to schemes of injustice." This follows from the greater option among the best characters which can be made, when fewer representatives represent larger constituencies. There is still a third reason, arising from the interaction of the two previous ones. The multiple interests, brought into contact (and conflict) by the principle of representation in the large republic, tend to cancel each other out by their very number and variety. They offer the representatives the opportunity of greater freedom in representing their constituencies—greater freedom from the local views of their constituents —by the variety of combinations which are possible, of local interests here with local interests there, and hence of local interests everywhere with the public interest. This opportunity, combined with the more elevated characters of the representatives themselves, is the basis of the optimism expressed by Madison in *The Federalist.* However, not only does this theory fail to consider political parties as we know them, but it cannot operate in the manner proposed by Madison in the presence of such parties. For it implies a certain community among the representatives of the large republic, as the most elevated characters in the entire union, brought together to reconcile and harmonize the selfish interests of their somewhat less morally elevated constituents. These representatives will be sufficiently divided by the fidelity to local interests and attachments demanded by the popular principle. To divide them further by a party label *within* the legislature, a label which will cause them to vote for or against a measure for a reason apart from that of local views, would compound, rather than simplify, the difficulties naturally inherent in the operation of the representative principle.

Against this theoretical background consider the main elements in the original federalist program. That program was based upon the premise that centrifugal forces would naturally be stronger than centripetal ones. The political motive in all of Hamilton's financial measures was to create a national economic interest. It was not simply to cement the wealthy classes to the central government; it was to create a class influential in every community whose "local" interest was national rather than sectional or parochial, and which would act on the representatives in a manner favorable to what their more "elevated" characters would wish. The promotion of industry was seen not only as a policy to increase wealth, but as a means of promoting exchanges between the localities of the union in such a way as to break down local feeling. Internal improvements by the national government were seen in the same light as a national bank and national debt. The improvement of transportation would assist in breaking down local barriers that were props to local feelings. The cap stone of all federalist ideas was Washington's great idea of a national university. The following is from his last annual address to Congress:

> Amongst the motives to such an Institution, the assimilation of the principles, opinions and manners of our Country men, by the common education of a portion of our Youth from every quarter, well deserves attention. The more homogeneous our Citizens can be made in these particulars, the greater will be our prospect of permanent Union; and a primary object of such a National Institution should be, the education of our Youth in the science of Government. In a Republic, what species of knowledge can be equally important?

79

and what duty more pressing on its Legislature, than to patronize a plan for communicating it to those, who are to be the future guardians of the liberties of the Country?[7]

"The assimilation of the principles, opinions and manners of our Country men" was the basic intention of all federalists, led by Washington, and of all federalist measures. This assimilation, however, had nothing in common with the uniformity of opinions, passions, and interests which Madison speaks of in the tenth *Federalist,* and which could be produced only by destroying liberty, although the Jeffersonians came to interpret it in that light. It was not meant to touch the diversity of interests as prompted at the grass roots by nature. It was meant rather to refine the gold in "a portion of our Youth from every quarter," so as further to elevate these naturally elevated characters, without which the representative principle was never expected to succeed.

Curiously enough, the idea of a national university was Jefferson's and Madison's, as well as Washington's, although Jefferson abandoned it in favor of a university for Virginia, and he and Madison came to believe that it would require a constitutional amendment for the federal government to have the power to establish it. But Jefferson's educational scheme for Virginia called for the "liberal education" to the highest level "without regard to wealth, birth or other accidental condition or circumstance" of those "whom nature hath endowed with genius and virtue," so that they might, when called to the offices which form and administer the laws, "be able to guard the sacred deposit of the rights and liberties of their fellow-citizens." An educational aristocracy, created out of the democratic principle of equality of opportunity, was the presupposition, among those who became federalists and republicans, of the idea of representative government. The bonds among the members of this class—the old school tie, American style—and the special allegiance its members would have to the Union, an allegiance intended in Jefferson's *original* idea, no less than in Washington's, would take the place subsequently taken by party loyalty.

[7] *Basic Writings of George Washington,* ed. Saxe Commins (New York: Random House, 1948) , p. 649.

# The Nature and Origin of the American Party System

In the original frame of government designed by the Founding Fathers, it is impossible to overestimate the importance in their calculations played by the general expectation that George Washington would be the first president. But Washington was a symbol as well as a man. He was a symbol of the unchallengeable moral virtue which would animate the highest national offices, and make men divided by parochial interests believe that these could be safely subordinated to an overriding national interest. Washington himself believed that the holders of such offices should, and could, work out their differences behind closed doors, much as the Constitutional Convention had done, and then present to the country a standard to which the wise and the good had already repaired, and which the rest of the country would certainly follow. Before condemning the naïveté of such a notion, as many present-day political scientists would do, let us remember that that is how the compromises of the Constitution *were* worked out. That, also, is how the Missouri Compromise was largely arrived at; and the Compromise of 1850 was an all-party arrangement, also arrived at largely *in camera.*

## VI

Let us recall then that the Declaration of Independence proposes an ideological problem. Only the consent of the enlightened can give rise to the just powers of government. In the eighteenth century, the devotees of liberty believed that the sun of enlightenment would one day finally dissipate the fogs of superstition that had so long enshrouded the government of man. Once the interests which supported privilege and absolutism had withered, opinion unfavorable to human rights would not arise, and there would be no cause for exclusion from political rights because of opinions. But there was no question that the enemies of liberty might not have any permanent and legitimate place within the regime of liberty. We today must recognize both the existence of the problem bequeathed to us by the Declaration and the danger inherent in it. That danger is even greater than the founders knew, because Nazism and Communism have taught us that foul doctrines hostile to human rights can spring from many causes that they did not anticipate, and among self-proclaimed friends of liberty no less than its avowed enemies. We must recognize the necessity of preventing the enemies of liberty from gaining power in the regime of liberty; but we must also recognize the extreme difficulty, and the danger, in the possible confusion of those whose interests differ from ours within that regime, and those who in truth stand outside of it. There is no formula for resolving such differences. They have in fact been confused, to some extent, at every point in our political history, save one. If slavery was right (as distinct from expedient), then free government itself was wrong. To find a middle ground between the principle of freedom and the principle of slavery "was as vain as the search for a man who should be neither a living man nor a dead man."

Our parties arose in the first instance because the Revolutionary adherents of the regime of liberty themselves fell out as to the appropriate means of reconciling the interests which they all understood such a regime would encourage. The parochial and selfish interests that they did expect gave rise to differences as to how those interests were to be reconciled, which they did not expect. Utopian expectations on both sides, expectations sheltered by the towering prestige of Washington, engendered on both sides ideological suspicions of those they held responsible for their disappointment. Neither side believed in monarchy or democracy (as democracy was defined in the eighteenth century), but distrust soon led one side to call the other "monocrats," and the other to retort "democrats." Still, it was the Jeffersonians alone who, in my judgment, constituted a political party, in a sense recognizable today. For it was the Jeffersonians alone who deliberately re-created the spirit of 1776, with the rhetoric of 1776, and employed the popular organizational techniques of 1776, to present themselves as the preservers of a popular republic against its enemies. Even the best federalists were rather technicians in government, whose morale depended upon the "aegis" of Washington and who passed with his passing.

The extent to which the two-party system in America depends upon the idea of one-party government may be indicated by the history of party nomenclature. Both parties which survive today bear parts of the name of that first great party. Jefferson's party was at first called simply the "republican" party. Later it took as a badge of honor, what was at first an opprobrious epithet, and called itself the "democratic-republican" party. In the era of Jackson, "republican" was dropped. But when the anti-Nebraska party was looking for a name, after 1854, it revived the original name of the Jeffersonians, to indicate that the republicans alone preserved the faith of the original Jeffersonian mission. "Federalists" and "Whigs," names which in themselves do not refer to principles, are no longer with us, along with the less significant names of many less significant parties. But we are today nearly all Democrats or Republicans, because the democratic-republican party was the first and, in a sense, the only party this country has known.

CHARLES M. HARDIN

●

# EMERGENT DEFECTS IN THE AMERICAN CONSTITUTIONAL SYSTEM*

As in all working constitutional democracies, so in the United States, political parties emerge as organizations aimed at controlling government—its personnel, its power, and its purposes. In free regimes, parties are the operating political agents, creating alike the present government and (equally important) its organized opposition and the potential future government. Parties grow up out of the class, sectional, ethnic, and interest groupings of communities; they are informed by the political ethos—the customs, aspirations, expectations, and working political theories that together provide the impulse and direction of community politics; they are shaped by the institutional processes, some written and some not, that organize and distribute political power. In turn, parties have an influence upon the political groupings, the ethos, and the institutions of communities. Together, this interconnected operating whole of parties, groups, ethos, and institutions makes the living constitution. In the United States it is manifest in a government of unexampled powers which nevertheless remains drastically limited in its purposes and methods. Never has the principle of constitutional democracy shone more brightly than now—in contrast to the totalitarian alternatives. Never before has the adequacy of its underlying institutions been so abruptly and so ultimately challenged.

* Research for the study from which this paper was drawn was largely conducted during 1960 when, as a member of the faculty of political science of The University of Chicago, the writer held the Ford Foundation Research Professorship.

Suddenly the American constitutional system exhibits glaring faults. The rise of Sino-Soviet communism, the uprush of nuclear and rocket weaponry, the population crescendo, the explosion of new nations, the revolution of rising expectations, and the internationalization of politics—all these compel us to reexamine our fundamental political processes.

Many of the salient features of our politics that together formed the supportable "price of union" as recently as, say, 1950 now show as weaknesses in the world struggle for survival. Our calendar elections and the interminable campaigns they engender now offer potential enemies recurrent opportunities to harass us. We can ill afford a system which produces a president who is virtually unreplaceable for four years regardless of whether his political abilities sustain themselves throughout the period. The general organization of American politics still rests on a major assumption that is no longer tenable: that our central political problem is to resolve peacefully a myriad of domestic issues. The separation of legislative from executive powers; the multiplication of power centers in Congress; the built-in vulnerability of government to local, sectional, and group interests; the hyperbolic fractionalization of American politics—all these cripple the nation's efforts to concert its policies, to order its priorities, and to carry through the hard national choices on which survival depends. Finally, our inherited institutions prevent the emergence of a stable, focused public opinion which can sustain that steady concentration of thought, effort, and will which world politics now exacts of the most powerful constitutional democracy.

These defects in the American political system should compel the most searching appraisal of its fundamentals since 1787. Unfortunately, most, if not all, of them are immune from correction by tacit agreement or by modification of unwritten laws; rather, they are firmly imbedded in the written constitution itself. The first task for this generation is to decide whether the defects are grave enough to require fundamental constitutional change, as this essay will argue.

## CALENDAR ELECTIONS

Calendar elections were not dangerous during our protracted insulation from world politics. After 1864, when the Union was nearly broken by the coincidence of a presidential election with a climactic threat to survival, this country had no presidential campaign during a major war until 1944. Thirty-one months after World War I began we entered it. Twenty-six months separated the outbreak of World War II in Europe from Pearl Harbor. If the third war comes, we will be involved in the first minutes.

During 1944 Winston Churchill, disturbed by the rise of Russian power, wanted to invest as much of Europe as possible. He proposed an attack across the Istrian peninsula toward Vienna. President Roosevelt demurred. "For purely political considerations over here, I should never survive even a slight setback in 'Overlord' if it were known that fairly large forces had been diverted." Over Churchill's protests Roosevelt also decided not to oppose Russia on the issue of aiding General Bor Komorowski's tragic revolt in Warsaw (August–October, 1944). Again, Roosevelt was apparently heavily influenced by the imminence of the presidential election.[1]

In March of 1948 the United States called for a temporary trusteeship for Palestine, in lieu of the proposed partition then under debate. "Thomas E. Dewey and other Republican leaders immediately attacked the administration [and this] put the Jew-Moslem issue squarely into the Presidential elections of 1948. . . ." When the British mandate expired on May 14, Ben Gurion proclaimed the new state of Israel which Truman immediately recognized "to anticipate the demand of Dewey or another Republican for the action. . . ."[2]

Again, in 1948 the Russians blockaded Berlin in June. By waiting until October they might have exploited the passions aroused by the campaign and tested whether an administration widely predicted to be on the verge of extinction could act vigorously. In 1950 congressional elections fell at a propitious time in the Korean War. Six weeks later the elections could have resulted in the public repudiation of the use by the United States of limited war as a tool of policy—or, alternatively, they

---

[1] Both examples and the quotation are taken from William P. Gerberding, "Franklin D. Roosevelt's Conception of the Soviet Union in World Politics," (unpublished Ph.D. dissertation, University of Chicago, 1959), Chapter IX.

[2] Arthur Krock, *New York Times*, July 17, 1958.

might have propelled us toward all-out war "at the wrong time, in the wrong place, and against the wrong enemy." In 1952 the stalemated slaughter in Korea fattened the Eisenhower landslide and produced what Samuel Lubell thought might well be the first in a series of violent electoral swings in which the public wrath is vented now on this, now on that, party. In 1954 the Chinese Reds could have tormented us more skillfully by inflaming the Formosan straits a few months earlier—a trick which they may have learned by 1958 when Quemoy and Matsu were brought to boil during the congressional campaign. The sharp domestic criticism of the Dulles-Eisenhower response seemed to be confirmed at the polls. In 1956, on the other hand, it was our friends rather than our potential enemies who synchronized the Suez adventure with our quadrennial government-making.

The major flaw in fixed calendar elections, the weapon that they add to our enemies' already formidable arsenal, could be largely removed by a system requiring elections in five years but at the discretion of the government—which is to say, the party—in power. *In extremis,* this alternative would permit the postponement of general elections as Britain has done during both world wars without sacrificing the essentials of constitutional government. Moreover, the alternative system would remove or ameliorate other flaws which, for lack of space, can only be suggested here: the protraction of campaigns, the grievous physical strains that they impose on candidates, their exorbitant monetary costs, and the undue vent they give to emotionalism, a necessary element of democratic politics, but one readily capable of exaggeration at the expense of reason, also a necessary element.

### An Irremovable President

The second flaw in the present constitution is its failure to provide for the removal of a president who has become *politically* disabled—that is, a leader who can no longer sense that the nation is in mortal danger or, if he can sense it, who can no longer bring himself to do what he knows should be done, or who no longer has the real authority to act. This imperfection requires some discussion because it has been obscured by stress upon another undoubted flaw: the difficulty of replacing a physically or mentally disabled president.

## Charles M. Hardin

The British experience in both world wars is instructive. Asquith was hale and hearty in 1916 when Lloyd George replaced him as Prime Minister. "Asquith . . . had shown in his handling of the Parliament Act all the gifts that peace could demand of a Constitutional statesman. [He] had secured that we entered the war united and not divided. . . . But the qualities that could launch us smoothly into the war could not teach us to weather its storms. . . ."[3] As a war Prime Minister, "Asquith was poor, while Lloyd George was a success."[4]

Neville Chamberlain was healthy when he was forced to give way to Winston Churchill in May, 1940. The Labor Party, which had refrained from obstruction and from "embarrassing the conduct of the war by inconvenient debates," went into opposition with the fall of Norway. Although Chamberlain unfortunately and mistakenly called on his "friends" for support, the fact of Labor opposition, the defection of 33 Conservatives, and the abstention of 60 Conservatives eventually brought on his resignation. "L. S. Amery, a friend and colleague over many years, borrowed Cromwell's ringing words to the Long Parliament: 'You have sat too long here for any good you have been doing. . . . In the name of God, go!' "[5]

Such are the problems of modern government that a good and even an excellent leader in one situation may miserably fail in another. "At the top there are great simplifications," [wrote Winston Churchill]. "An accepted leader has only to be sure of what it is best to do, or at least to have made up his mind about it. The loyalties which center on number one are enormous. If he trips he must be sustained. If he makes mistakes they must be covered. If he sleeps he must not be wantonly disturbed. If he is no good he must be pole-axed."[6] It should be clear that we have to provide for removal not only in physical but also in political disability, that of the two the latter presents the more difficult

[3] K. B. Smellie, *A Hundred Years of English Government* (2d ed.; London: Gerald Duckworth and Co., Ltd., 1950), pp. 174–79.

[4] W. Ivor Jennings, *The British Constitution* (Cambridge, England: University Press, 1942), p. 162.

[5] *Ibid.*, pp. 191–92, and R. T. McKenzie, *British Political Parties* (London: Wm. Heinemann, Ltd., 1955), p. 47.

[6] *The Second World War*, Vol. II, *Their Finest Hour* (Boston: Houghton Mifflin Co., 1949), p. 15.

problem, and that the act of removal in either case is greatly facilitated by—and may be possible only with—strong party government. Somehow, we must provide ourselves with a constitutional way to change horses in midstream.

## PUBLIC POLICY FORMATION

The tendency to divide and splinter public policy formation and execution, built into the original constitution by the separation of powers and staggered congressional elections, has been strengthened by the development of decentralized parties, the proliferation of power centers (including public agencies, congressional blocs, and allied pressure groups), and such conventions as senatorial courtesy and the seniority system in Congress: these characteristics and developments are reinforced by the corresponding patterns of political behavior that have developed around the system.

The pyramiding demands for more vigorous and more coordinated public policies will not be met by our inherited, fragmentized system; rather, they require a new system of government in which centralized, policy-oriented parties play a central role. Clearly, this is not an argument which—any more than the rebuttal to it—can be "proved." But both sides of the debate should be vigorously developed.

The counterargument is that in exigencies the American polity rises to the occasion and produces the Reciprocal Trade Agreement Act or the Marshall Plan or the vast and effective network of contracts and arrangements that has effectively hitched the scientific community to the national purpose.

In the face of this massive denial, how does one argue that radical changes are needed? The defenders of the present system have failed to gauge our past performance or our future exigencies. Historically, we were able to get along with minimal national government until the great depression, which the struggles of the New Deal met with only indifferent success, as the unemployment rolls of the 1930's witness. Then we had the war and the sustained postwar prosperity. Now we face new challenges that ought to give us pause.

Consider economic policy. Inflation has been checked since 1951, and deflations have been reversed so that no deep depressions have developed. But even with a sustained high level of activity the unemployment rate has stubbornly refused to fall below 5.5 per cent of the labor force, and this figure hides the fact that a considerable number of people come to be omitted from, or take themselves out of, the labor force; and it also obscures the much heavier incidence of unemployment among the young, the nonwhites, and the relatively poorly educated. Thus during the four years 1958–1962 we experienced an annual net gain of only 1,000,000 new jobs. But the Council of Economic Advisers estimated that to reduce unemployment to 4 per cent during 1963 would require an additional 1,100,000 jobs, *plus* perhaps 800,000 more jobs for persons who would then reappear in the labor market, *plus* 1,200,000 jobs for the annual addition of young people to the labor force during the year, *plus* an unknown number of jobs needed to replace those eliminated by automation. In short, three and one-half to four times as many new jobs would have to be created as the annual average of the last four years. And because of the rapid rise of numbers in the labor force (the babies of the 1940's coming of working age) and the increased trends toward automation, each year for perhaps ten years will require substantial expansion of the number of jobs if we are to keep unemployment at 4 per cent. But if we succeed in this, we will encourage inflationary tendencies that have been held in check in a slack economy.

To help meet the problems implicit in the last paragraph, the national government will have to work largely indirectly, through regulation of the supply of money, through management of the government debt, through taxation, and through governmental spending. All this requires a co-ordination in policy-making and execution which is very difficult to achieve in a government that divides these functions between the executive and the legislative and then redivides them within each of the major branches. On the executive side, the Treasury, the Bureau of the Budget, and the Council of Economic Advisers are involved; on the legislative, the Appropriations Committees, the House Ways and Means Committee, the Senate Finance Committee, the Banking and Currency Committee, and the Joint Economic Committee. Finally, the Federal Reserve Board is considerably independent of both the executive and Congress.

We also need much more thoroughgoing appraisals of the balance of federal expenditures among the various claimants. To say nothing of the continued outlays for the military or for the space program, we can properly call in question the funds budgeted for, say, agriculture as against education, or for rivers and harbors, water power and reclamation, and related fields, as against funds for urban development.

Let us also note the conflicts between foreign and domestic policy. Historically, the Smoot-Hawley Tariff, the Chinese and Japanese Exclusion Acts, and the Silver Purchase Act have been among those with very unfortunate effects upon our foreign policy. On numerous occasions between 1890 and 1948 our tariffs and quotas to protect American sugar interests have upset the Cuban economy. Among other items that may be cited are the protection of petroleum, of textiles, and of lead and zinc; the subsidized exportation of domestic agricultural surpluses; the Walters–McCarran Act; and the repeated tendency of Congress to deal with technical assistance as a short-run problem. On all these, at the very least, we need the most penetrating inquiries to inform judgments whether (as this writer believes) the tendency of the American system to give domestic issues priority over the national interest in foreign politics has reached dangerous proportions.

Before leaving this area of discussion, let us note the argument that if we manage to reorganize our government so as greatly to increase the role of centrally organized and responsible political parties this will deliver us into the hand of the experts. It can safely be retorted that we are in their hands now. Don K. Price's "deeper reason" for writing *Government and Science* "was a notion that . . . the development of public policy owed less in the long run to . . . conflict among political parties and social or economic pressure groups than to the more objective processes of research and discussion among professional groups." In every policy area familiar to the writer there is now a heavy component of expertise, including that contributed by large numbers of Congressmen. What is too often lacking is that contribution of the political art that transcends the discovery of compromises that simply insure a sufficient response to the affected interests so that government may bumble along.

## Charles M. Hardin

THE SPECTER OF IDEOLOGICAL DIVISION

The prospect of pitting two nationally organized parties against each other dismays Ernest Griffith and Edward Banfield who predict that political issues will then become divisively explosive. Griffith argues, in *Congress: Its Contemporary Role,* that a century ago, in an age of relatively few and simple issues, systematic partisan alignments might have presented voters with rather clear-cut choices that were at once understandable and politically adequate (that is, sufficiently expressive of the contemporary conflicts of interest and purpose). Now, he says, our complex society has multiplied issues until no majority can be found which can concert a stand on enough of them—a stand in clear opposition to the similarly concerted position of the opposition party —to make elections on the basis of centralized, disciplined, issue-oriented parties feasible.

With respect, Dr. Griffith's argument seems to be based upon a common misconstruction of the problem, which is *not* to give the voter an unequivocal choice between two opposed and internally consistent programs (liberal free trade versus conservative protectionism, for example). The objective, rather, is to produce a government that can meet the political problems of the day while still being accountable to the electorate. Today's political problems have suddenly sharpened and deepened at the same time that they have become international. They also show themselves to be interrelated so that they need to be met by policies which form much more integrated programs. For example, despite our tremendous wealth, demands upon the budget loom so large that we can no longer safely provide "a little plum for everyone." Rather, we need to subject spending to much closer scrutiny than before—and this requires more centralized power in government. Again, our logrolling politics, which we have so long and luxuriously afforded, now compromises the national interest by reducing the necessary maneuverability of government.

An accountable government, sufficiently centralized to develop the requisite programmatic approach to present problems, requires support of a party that agrees to stand or fall together on its general performance. What other source of political support is there? But it is false to forecast two parties opposing each other on oversimplified, completely contradictory, and internally rigid (if consistent) programs. Laski raised this specter in *Parliamentary Government in England,* only to be refuted by events. In England, rather, the two political parties have drawn closer together so that the images of both become blurred.

There are, however, more subtle implications in Griffith's argument which Banfield makes explicit.[7] Banfield agrees with Charles E. Merriam that "The adequate organization of modern metropolitan areas is one of the great unsolved problems of modern politics." But he argues that the problem is not merely one "of creating organization for effective planning and administration. It is also—and perhaps primarily—one of creating, or of maintaining, organization for the effective management of conflict arising from the growing cleavages of race and class."

Certainly this is one of the most powerful arguments for decentralized political parties. In developing his position, Banfield argues for businesslike parties that hold their active, working members essentially by material rewards—by jobs that are more remunerative and prestigeful in direct proportion to the political effectiveness of the party worker concerned, namely, his ability to get out the vote. Given parties run by such officers, vexing problems can be solved, if at all, more easily and with less violence because they are handled by men dependent for their livelihood on their success in getting things done. Contrarily, parties built upon ideals rather than on patronage and held together by principles rather than material interests will turn every fight into an Armageddon and, if the issues are grave enough, will destroy the community rather than patch it together with peaceful compromises.

The answer to this argument is to concede that Banfield has brilliantly stated a profound political problem, but then to argue that the problem will be no worse and may even be better with centralized, disciplined, policy-oriented parties. Our present politics, with its decentralized, patronage-based parties, breeds violent ideological politics—witness the John Birch Society; the antisubversive campaigns in the states; the cry of Communism,

[7] "The Politics of Metropolitan Area Organization," *Midwest Journal of Political Science,* I (May, 1957), 90.

Korea, and Corruption in 1952; attacks upon economic royalists and malefactors of an earlier day; anti-Catholicism in 1928; and the "Know-Nothings." True enough, the English system has produced its bitter campaigns revolving around the seemingly fatal (if sometimes false) confrontation of irreconcilable principles—the Zinoviev letter in 1924 is the prime example. But on the whole the British record compares well with ours, partly because campaigns are shorter, but chiefly because British political parties have more to attack and defend in terms of specific policies—and are, therefore, driven less than our parties to questioning the morals and loyalty of opponents.

## Federalism and Heterogeneity as Obstacles to Party Government

"Parties, because they seek to control the government, are structured in accordance with governmental structure. . . . If the government is divided federally and functionally, the effort to control it will be similarly dispersed."[8] The admonition implicit in this statement is clearly applicable to the United States. Our parties have been essentially loose federations of state organizations. Even within the states the parties have been much more concerned with the control of nominations, of offices, and of patronage than they have with the development of systematic and integrated state political policy. But if the needs of the times call for different kinds of parties, what are the chances? V. O. Key, Jr., has advocated strengthening party government within the states and suggested some steps which might create favorable conditions for this eventuality.[9] But the concern here is with the wisdom and possibility of creating an effective national system of party government. Is federalism an effective obstacle to the development of party government at both the central and state (or provincial) levels? Comparative analysis suggests that it is not. Rather, the parliamentary systems in both Canada and Australia show that federal government is in principle compatible with the emergence of responsible, policy-

[8] C. J. Friedrich, *Constitutional Government and Democracy* (Boston: Ginn & Co., 1950), p. 419.
[9] *American State Politics* (New York: Alfred A. Knopf, 1956), p. 282.

oriented party government at both the national and the state levels.[10]

But it still may be that the basic social cleavages of the American community will not permit the development of party government. Federalism is held to be appropriate for political communities with sharp internal differences (ethnic, religious, or cultural) which are geographically based—Quebec, the American South, and the German, French, and Italian cantons of Switzerland are examples. In *The Price of Union,* Herbert Agar has urged that the "diverse climates and economic interests and social habits and racial and religious backgrounds" inevitably give American politics its parochial stamp. Agar believes that the divisions of the American community are too various, conflicting, and kaleidoscopic to be organizable in a two-party system stable enough to discharge the task of modern government.

Three points may be made in reply. First, Agar himself confessed to grave doubts whether the American system that he had praised so eloquently will be able to cope with future problems.[11] Second, the argument usually explains that Britain is sufficiently homogenized to support party government whereas the United States is not, but this ignores both the facts of British life and the role of the parties themselves in shaping British opinion to conform with the needs of party government.[12] Third, social, economic, and governmental developments in the United States show that many issues which might have broken party unity in an earlier day are no longer sharp enough to do so. Prohibition is gone. The tariff is no longer a sectional issue. Eastern metropolitan Democrats have accepted agricultural price supports and large programs for Western water- and power-development;

[10] David B. Truman, "Federalism and the Party System," in A. W. Macmahon, *et al., Federalism: Mature and Emergent* (Garden City, N.Y.: Doubleday & Co., 1955), p. 126. Gwendolyn M. Carter, "The Commonwealth Overseas: Variation on a British Theme," in Sigmund Neumann (ed.), *Modern Political Parties* (Chicago: University of Chicago Press, 1956), p. 95. Louise Overacker, *The Australian Party System* (New Haven: Yale University Press, 1952), p. 327.

[11] Herbert Agar, *The Price of Union* (Boston: Houghton Mifflin Co., 1950), pp. 279-80, fn.; cf. *The Price of Power* (Chicago: University of Chicago Press, 1957), *passim.*

[12] Samuel H. Beer, "Group Representation in Britain and the United States," *The Annals,* CCCXIX (September, 1958), 130-40.

small town and rural Democrats of the West and South have accepted minimum-wage legislation, governmental guarantees of labor's right to bargain collectively, and social-security programs. Republicans of all sections have had, in general, to acquiesce in similar policies. The election of a Catholic to the presidency indicates that one clear source of internal division which was highly divisive in 1928 has been mitigated, although the issue over equal assistance to parochial schools still is a formidable obstacle to massive federal aid to education. With one exception, the United States does not seem to be plagued by the nemesis of postwar French politics: the failure to establish a majority on any two of the salient national political issues.[13]

The remaining divisive issue is race relations, and no one can depreciate its gravity. As Samuel Lubell notes, the South "is the great exposed flank of the Democratic Party."[14] It is difficult to believe that a national Democratic Party could presently concert a program which dealt with civil rights in a manner acceptable to both its Southern and its Northern-Western wings. The writer concedes that this one issue, even if all other factors were propitious, would probably prevent the United States from achieving party government now. But the constitutional reform for which this paper argues is the task of at least a generation, during which both the position and the location of Negroes will continue to change, hopefully in ways that will make the race relations problem more amenable to party government.

## The Ethos

Let us assume that a considerable shift in the American governmental system toward emphasizing the role of disciplined, centralized, policy-oriented parties will not foment dangerous ideological cleavages. Let us also assume that such a shift is compatible with federalism and will not fail in its consummation because of the heterogeneity of American politics. These are negative obstacles; that their importance is diminishing is a necessary condition for the success of party government. But it may not be a sufficient condition. There may also be necessary the

[13] Philip Williams, *Politics in Post-War France* (London: Longmans, Green & Co., 1954).

[14] Samuel Lubell, "Future of the Negro Voter in the United States," *Journal Negro Education*, XXVI, No. 3 (Summer, 1957), 408–17.

emergence of the positive popular consensus that will support party government as a means of obtaining or approximating, through government action, certain conditions of economic and social life that are deeply and widely held to be both desirable and legitimate. In a penetrating analysis, Samuel H. Beer objects to any focus on groups and interests which ignores their cultural context. "In the study of American and British politics, such neglect means passing over important elements of consensus which are shared throughout the political system and involve not only the 'rules of the game,' but also positive social and political values."

Professor Beer finds that the American consensus is in the tradition of John Locke in its acceptance of "democratic capitalism." The British consensus, on the other hand, roots deeply in an organic view of society: preponderant groups in both major parties would "agree with Burke on that un-American proposition that 'government is a contrivance of human wisdom to provide for human wants,' and that 'men have a right that those wants shall be provided for by that wisdom.' "[15]

For the sake of the argument let us accept the juxtaposition of Locke and Burke and ask only: Is it true that the American consensus is so essentially negative that it would not support a role for American parties equally vital to that which Beer ascribes to British parties as "not only coalitions of interest groups, but also [as] bearers of values of the classes and of the collectivity?" We can point to the formidable degree of acceptance of government shown by the success of a self-administered income tax in the United States—96 per cent of the estimated taxable income being reported and paid upon by individuals in some 96,000,000 tax returns. Despite the draft riots in the Civil War, we can point to the success of selective service in this century. If these are acknowledged as signs that Americans will, indeed, accept modern government but are dismissed as irrelevant respecting any deep American propensities to view government as providing for human wants, we may cite other events. First, the evidence is compelling that Americans now look positively to government as the architect of prosperity—the Employment Act

[15] "Pressure Groups and Parties in Britain," *American Political Science Review*, L, No. 1 (March, 1956), 2, 21–22.

of 1946 is only one example. Second, there is much evidence of positive demands that both parties must heed for government assurance of social security. Third, there is the demand that government find "answers" to specific but very broad social and economic problems such as agricultural maladjustment, urban redevelopment, and the conservation and development of natural resources. In all these, "government" means, essentially, Washington.

The evidence seems to show that the American ethos is not an obstacle to party government but rather that the consensus on "positive social and political values" would support it. At the same time, the American ethos lacks political institutions which fix the attention of statesmen and citizens alike on the common and general interest. In the United States political opinion is essentially focused by our institutions upon the immediate interest—workers on wages, farmers on prices, stockmen on grazing privileges, lumbermen on the accessibility of timber, miners on protection of the domestic market, and so on. Members of such interests can become concerned about broader questions such as policy toward Latin America or toward India or respecting education or civil defense. But they know less about the large questions; the quick dollar-in-the-pocket aspect is usually missing, and their attention wavers. The effect of this lack of a steady focus is worsened by the looming problems of policy integration already noted. True, there are some organizations like the League of Women Voters which help direct the attention of some citizens to questions of general interest; but what is lacking is membership in policy-oriented parties that can effectively link the special interests of citizens with their proper national and international concerns.

There are, indeed, broad, often vague, sometimes compulsive sentiments: devotion to saving natural resources, to securing the offshore oil for Texas, to ridding the schools of supposed subversives, to smiting labor—or the cattle barons—or Wall Street —or aliens—or the Jews, to improving education, to reducing floods, or to fighting disease. Some of these sentiments seem stronger than others, more persistent, and politically more significant, especially those associated with shared economic interests, such as the perennial interest of the frontiersman in cheap money, or the interest of workers in wages, employment security, and "control of the job," or the interest of farmers in parity. In addition, religion and national derivation produce political cohesions and clashes; and with us the most profound cleavages are rooted in race relations.

Our political problem is to produce out of the welter of local interests, sentiments, and political differences a common and steady attention upon the great national issues. All the conflicts of interest and purpose must express themselves in a free government; but if the community is to endure, these conflicts must be informed by a grasp of the state of the union in this perilous century and they must be channeled to support the great national exertions now demanded of us.

We need to work toward political institutions which make programmatic policies, which identify the effect of local and particular policies on great national concerns, and which force a consideration of alternative policies and expenditures. The effective political base for this kind of policy-making process must be found in national, centralized, disciplined, and policy-oriented political parties—parties, membership in which can stiffen the resistance of congressmen against the often irresistible constituent interests; and parties in which citizens as members can find both an empowering and a restraining experience that is emotionally and intellectually satisfying. Given such policy-oriented parties, citizens will have a standard by which to examine the thousand appeals to sentiment that constantly bombard them: what is the party's position in this matter? Something may be lost in spontaneity, individuality, and the multiplication of appeals to interest and sentiment; but in this century more will be gained in responsibility—in sensing a share in the concerted and steady national policies that survival demands.

### CONCLUSIONS

The conclusions of this paper were stated in the opening paragraphs. All constitutions are in large part political accidents, but ours was set in being in many of its essential aspects by a great act of statesmanship in 1787. Successful as the constitutional experience has been, the system has now produced serious faults which can be corrected only by conscious change. What the United States needs is a constitution-building generation, and the great task of current political science is to inform it.

# Charles M. Hardin

Central to the task of informing policy is a thorough examination of the alternative of party government. If calendar elections have become dangerous, the only apparent substitute is to require elections within a fixed period but to develop institutions which permit the exact time of the election to be set by the government of the day. The only known and working model that we have for this is made by the leaders of the majority party. Again, if we are to provide for replacing politically inadequate presidents, the only recourse seems to be through party government. On the question whether the American form of government can produce a sufficiently integrated approach to policy formation or, to state the question more exactly in terms of the intent of this chapter, on the question whether party government would produce a better integration than we now have, the evidence is less clear. An excellent case can be made that we are presently falling short of the level we need to attain, but the case for the superior alternative remains conjectural. Here the question could be usefully illuminated by a comparative analysis much more searching than any now available of the American and British constitutions.[16]

Finally, consider the question of which system, the American or the British, better provides for the emergence of a responsible public opinion. The writer believes that the weight of informed comment favors the British system. Samuel H. Beer has written that in comparison with the British both American parties and pressure groups are weak, but his general interpretation is laudatory of Britain's success in both permitting and even encouraging the representation of interests while still managing to focus and discipline them as the public interest requires. W. Ivor Jennings finds that much British legislation "is derived from

[16] Consider the Labor Government in postwar Britain. Having over-extended itself in 1945-46, having pushed its program too rapidly, the Labor Government was somewhat slow to apprehend the seriousness of inflation until some two months after the sterling crisis of 1947. But then the Government moved speedily and vigorously, trenching "deeply held objectives" and running counter to "powerful pressures" in its own ranks and in the trade unions. "Yet party and interest groups were convinced, or resisted, or sometimes appeased by moderate concessions, and a government which was committed by its principles to large scale spending carried out one of the most successful fights against inflation of any country during the post-war period." Samuel H. Beer, "Great Britain: From Governing Elite to Organized Mass Parties," in Sigmund Neumann (ed.), *Modern Political Parties*, p. 53.

organized interests . . . [that] most of it is amended on the representation of such interests, and . . . [that] often parliamentary opposition is in truth the opposition of interests." He also declares that the "national interest is an amalgam of hundreds of group interests"; but it is clear from his context that among the numerous groups to which he refers he ascribes the greatest weight to the general electorate.[17] Jennings also opts for government in the public interest (that is, the regime of a firm, identifiable and powerful government which rules in accordance with "the wishes of the people") in preference to government by pressure groups—and he makes his opinion clear that the British system more nearly than the American approximates this ideal.[18]

R. T. McKenzie acknowledges the powerful presence of interests in Britain, but notes that on occasion British governments "stand out boldly against the claim of pressure groups on the ground that to give way would be to betray the national interest."[19] Gerhard Loewenberg sums up his survey of "The British Constitution and the Structure of the Labor Party" by noting that Labor's rise to power required it "to be responsive to the entire electorate, to work with the parliamentary process, and to govern the nation effectively. . . ."[20] While expressing his forebodings about latent tendencies within the British system, Samuel E. Finer nevertheless believes that the British lobby "acts more soberly and responsibly" than its American counterpart.[21]

The writer does not say that these opinions are definitive but asserts only that the weight of the presently available analyses supports the conclusion that strong party government makes better provision both for the representation and for the discipline of public opinion than does the American system. Again, this subject invites the most thoroughgoing inquiry that political science can mount.

[17] *Parliament* (New York: Macmillan, 1940), pp. 179, 503.

[18] *The British Constitution*, especially p. 214 and pp. 227 ff.

[19] "Parties, Pressure Groups, and the British Political Process," *The Political Quarterly*, XXIX (January–March, 1958), especially 14–15. See also *British Political Parties*, Chapter X.

[20] *American Political Science Review*, LII, No. 3 (September, 1958), 790 and *passim*.

[21] *The Anonymous Empire* (London: Pall Mall Press, 1958), Chapter VII. See also S. E. Finer's "Transport Interests and the Road Lobby," *The Political Quarterly*, XXIX (January–March, 1958), 47 ff.

MORTON GRODZINS

●

# PARTY AND GOVERNMENT IN THE UNITED STATES*

How do American political parties affect the operation of the American government? The argument of this paper is that the parties are significant in preserving both the existence and form of the considerable measure of governmental decentralization that exists in the United States. The focus of attention is, therefore, upon the classic problem of a federal government: the distribution of power between the central and peripheral units. Yet there is little in what follows concerning formal, or constitutional, power relationships. The word "sovereignty" does not appear. Decisions of the Supreme Court are not emphasized. The concern of the paper is not juridical concepts or the sporadic umpiring of the courts, but the day-to-day pattern of who does what under whose influence; not the theoretical locus of supreme powers, but the actual extent of sharing of decision-making in legislation and administration among the central, state, and local governments.

## I. THE CAUSES OF DECENTRALIZATION

The nature of American political parties is only one of many causes of governmental decentralization.[1] The parties are not

*This article is an adaptation of a paper, "American Political Parties and the American System," published in *The Western Political Quarterly*, XIII, No. 4 (1960), 974–98, and is a product of the federalism workshop of the University of Chicago, a research and training program carried out with support from the Ford Foundation. For helpful criticism of an earlier draft, I am indebted to Kaspar D. Naegele, Harry H. Eckstein, and Lee Benson, all colleagues during 1958–59 at the Center for Advanced Study in the Behavioral Sciences.
[1] Because so many factors are involved, there is no invariable relationship between decentralized parties and decentralized government. No exam-

even the most important cause. But they provide an excellent point for focusing analysis on the issue of decentralization because they reflect and make operative other causal factors. Radical changes in the party system would imply radical changes in society and in constitutional practices, and would produce radical changes in the geographic distribution of governmental powers.

What are the other factors causing governmental decentralization? In the first place, it can easily be shown that the causal relationship between party and government is a reciprocal one. For example, many of the formal constitutional provisions that were established to prevent a majority faction from completely controlling the national government also militate against the organization of the majority faction itself. The substantial control over elections given to the states; the electoral college system (combined with the extraconstitutional nominating convention); the fixed terms for President, senators, and congressmen; the composition of the Senate; the amendment process; the appointment procedure and tenure for Supreme Court justices— these as well as other constitutional provisions can be said to "cause" party disunity. Directly and through the function of parties they also "cause" decentralized government.[2]

No formal amendment procedure is needed to alter many constitutional practices. But it is clearly not true that the Constitution is no longer important in establishing the distribution of power between the federal government and the states. The latitude of interpretation that is possible with respect to the interstate commerce clause cannot equally be applied elsewhere. The simple, clearly stated, unambiguous phrases—for example, the President "shall hold his office during the term of four years" —are subject to change only through the formal amendment

---

ples of decentralized parties in centralized governments come easily to mind. But the obverse situation—relatively centralized parties in relatively decentralized governments—occurs frequently. Canada and the Netherlands provide good examples.

[2] For relevant discussions see Herbert Wechsler, "The Political Safeguards of Federalism: The Role of the States in the Composition and Selection of the National Government," in Arthur W. Macmahon (ed.), *Federalism, Mature and Emergent* (New York: Doubleday, 1955), pp. 97–114; Austin Ranney and Willmoore Kendall, *Democracy and the American Party System* (New York: Harcourt, Brace, 1956), especially chap. 21.

processes. And it is this sort of constitutional statement that is at once an impediment to the tight organization of both government and parties. If the terms of the President and members of Congress were not so firmly defined in the Constitution, the power of party leaders to enforce discipline would be immeasurably increased. Similarly, state constitutional provisions, such as those providing for the independent election of state administrators and for the direct primaries in the nomination of candidates for the governor's office, have the effect of splintering state parties and, by extension, of impeding the development of structured national parties and national party government.[3] The parties become a chief avenue for the achievement of decentralized government. But governmental (here formal constitutional) factors are partially responsible for the manner in which parties are structured. So government causes the form of party; party causes the form of government.

Second, a wide range of factors not directly related to the party-government interrelationship contributes to governmental decentralization. One certainly is in the form of creed, the opinion of Americans, as molded by tradition and history, that places a high value on the grass roots, local initiative, and vigorous local institutions. Another is pride in locality and state, and allegiance to them, fostered by the nation's size, the different speeds of cultural and industrial development, and the varieties of regional, if not state, histories. The sheer wealth of the nation can also be shown as a cause of governmental decentralization. It renders possible the sharing of governmental largesse by many groups, including the state and local governments, provides leeway for experimentation and even waste, and renders unnecessary the tight organization of political power that is found when the support of one cause necessarily means the deprivation of another.

Other social and economic forces are important for the decentralized structure of American government. All of them may variously make themselves felt (1) directly on government; (2) directly on parties; (3) through parties on government; and (4) through government on parties. To take only the most obvious

[3] V. O. Key, *American State Politics: An Introduction* (New York: Knopf, 1956), especially chaps. 3, 4, and 7.

sort of example, the lack of deep, divisive schisms with respect to basic economic issues in the American society makes possible a viable government in which the executive is controlled by one party, the legislature by another. So social structure directly affects government. The same basic unity on economic matters allows parties to be only marginally unlike and permits members of one party to support the other party on many issues. So social structure affects parties and through parties affects government. Even more elaborate causal chains could be constructed if they served any useful purpose. In fact, they rarely do. The only point here is to make clear that many cultural factors are causal for both undisciplined parties and decentralized government. Reciprocally, it can also be shown that party and government processes reflect back on the culture. The open government and the open society are not separate entities.

Third, a cause of party disunity and governmental decentralization also exists in the mediating role that parties play between society, on the one hand, and government, on the other. This is a special case of the reciprocal influence of social factors and party organization. Norton Long has outlined, without providing the empirical evidence, the manner in which the present disunity of the parties serves significant social groups: businessmen and professional workers, farmers, ethnic groups, and state and local office-holders.[4] The argument, in brief, is that sizable population groups believe that they profit from the present organization of parties and that they might be deprived (or at least not equally indulged) if parties became more programmatic and unified. On the other hand, no easily organized, powerful groups are presently deprived, or believe they would be appreciably indulged, by greater unity. Proof of the argument involves one in difficult methodological problems. Yet it contains a fundamentally sound perception. If majority social groups in the country were convinced of the advantages of party unity, constitutional barriers might make the task of creating unified parties more difficult, but those barriers would hardly be controlling. Party disunity and governmental decentralization are

[4] Norton E. Long, "Party Government and the United States," *Journal of Politics*, XIII (May, 1951), 187–214. For historical evidence see Herbert Agar, *The Price of Union* (Boston: Houghton Mifflin, 1930).

in large measure the direct consequences of the rewards that they give to significant social groups.

Finally, within this picture of many overlapping and reciprocal causes of governmental decentralization, the parties themselves have an important role. They are not mere weather vanes moved by the shifting winds of law, ideology, wealth, and social structure. They supply breezes of their own. Members of Congress express their own will, as well as that of constituency groups, in their devotion to the seniority principle for committee assignments and the right of unlimited debate in the Senate. The state governors and other local party chiefs play roles that they would not play in a system of centralized parties, and it is to their personal and professional advantage to maintain those roles. Cash for careerists is one consequence of disunited parties. The system also distributes status and power to individuals whose upward mobility might otherwise be impossible. Issues of sociability, of personal ambition, of honest (and dishonest) graft, of the patronage of prestige, of intraparty institutional stability are all involved. In the view of those most concerned, these factors are inseparable from their view of the welfare of the nation, however narrow or exalted that view may be. The party-government relationship, in other words, can be understood as a closed system, with the parties standing as a relatively autonomous social force. Their undisciplined character is the product of their internal dynamics, as well as of other factors, and it contributes to the decentralization of the American government.

## II. The Parties as Decentralizers

### THE BASIC SHARING IN LEGISLATION

The parties contribute to governmental decentralization, first of all, by determining in legislation the basic sharing of functions between the federal government on the one hand, and state and local governments on the other. Lord Bryce described the "working relations" of the national and state governments in the following words:

> The characteristic feature and special interest of the American Union is that it shows us two governments covering the same ground, yet distinct and separate in their action. It is like a great factory where-

in two sets of machinery are at work, their revolving
wheels apparently intermixed, their bands crossing one
another, yet each set doing its own work without touching or hampering the other.[5]

Classic works are sometimes responsible for classic errors. Bryce
was wrong, even for the period of his own observations, in de-
scribing the federal government and the states as "each . . .
doing its own work without touching or hampering the other."
The American system is pre-eminently a system in which functions and responsibilities are shared among the federal, state,
and local governments.

The federal government's participation in what are usually
conceived to be state and local functions is widespread indeed.[6]
But it is not our concern here. That concern is with the sharing
of federal programs by the states and localities. And the first
point is the basic one that "federal law is generally interstitial in
its nature,"[7] limited in objective and in any given area of
service or regulation building upon the main body of legal relationships defined by state law. It is difficult to find any area of
federal law that is not affected in important ways by state law.
Federal criminal statutes utilize state standards in defining federal crimes. Federal licenses are not granted unless applicants
meet licensing requirements established by state laws. Federal
tax laws are largely concerned with property relationships
created and defined by the states. Substantive rights established
in federal statutes have their enforcement left largely or wholly
to the states (though in exceptional cases Congress gives exclusive jurisdiction to the federal courts). Even in fields that on
their face concern exclusive federal spheres of action—that of
patents, for example—the mixture of law occurs. Patent laws do
not displace either the police or tax functions of the states, and
patent rights are subordinate to a given state's authority over
property within its limits.

[5] James Bryce, *The American Commonwealth* (London: Macmillan,
1890), I, 318.
[6] A simple listing of *Federal Services to Cities and Towns* by Robert H.
Blundred and Donoh W. Hanks, Jr., covers more than seventy pages and
ranges from "abbatoirs" and "accounting" to "zoning" and "zoo administration" (Chicago: American Municipal Association, 1950).
[7] Henry M. Hart, Jr., and Herbert Wechsler, *The Federal Courts and
the Federal System* (Brooklyn: Foundation Press, 1953), p. 435.

Examples of this sort could be multiplied endlessly. The important task is to understand how the American parties operate to produce this characteristic mixture of American law. Now, as in the first days of the republic, the local as opposed to the national orientation of most members of the national Congress leads to legislation that gives important responsibilities to states and localities.

The entire development of grant-in-aid programs generally supports the sharing hypothesis. The grant device from this perspective allows the federal government to utilize its purse powers while sharing with the states important responsibilities in program definition and administration. Two specific examples will demonstrate the process. These are "hard cases." The hard case as a method of analysis means choosing those data—or those events or problems—which seem most likely *not* to support the hypothesis being considered. The National Airport Act of 1946 and the unemployment insurance provisions of the Social Security Act of 1935 are hard cases with respect to the sharing hypothesis because there existed compelling reasons for establishing both programs without state participation.

The issue that vexed Congress with respect to the postwar airport bill was a direct sharing question: should local governments, particularly large cities, deal directly with the Civil Aeronautics Administration or should the flow of applications and funds between large cities and the CAA be "channeled" through state agencies? The cities, as represented by Mayor Fiorello LaGuardia of New York and the United States Conference of Mayors, supported direct city-federal negotiations; the states through the Governors' Conference demanded channeling. An impartial observer, if one could be found, would almost certainly have concluded that the cities had the better case. The states had few and rudimentary airport authorities and contributed from 1933 through 1945 less than 1 per cent of total national airport expenditures. Federal funds were preponderant (75 per cent), the federal-local pattern then existing had proved successful, and federal administrative officers testified that, for larger airports, they preferred to deal directly with local authorities.

The Governors' Conference took a strong stand in favor of

channeling,[8] and the Senate version of the bill was amended so as to channel all federal aid to airports through state agencies. The amendment was proposed by Republican Senator Owen Brewster of Maine, a former governor and former chairman of the executive committee of the Governors' Conference. The roll-call vote on the Brewster mandatory channeling amendment was as follows:

|  | Republicans | Democrats | Progressives | Total |
|---|---|---|---|---|
| Yea | 24 | 15 | 1 | 40 |
| Nay | 7 | 26 | | 33 |

Party influence is apparent, but party control plainly not: the Republicans, a clear minority in the Senate of the 79th Congress, could not have won without the fifteen Democratic defectors and thirteen Democratic non-voters. The crucial factor bringing victory to the states was not party affiliation. It was the conduct of senators who had once served as state governors. Sixteen former governors voted. Twelve were in favor of the amendment. Party identification made little difference: five of six Republican former governors and seven of ten Democratic ones supported the channeling amendment. Whereas 52 per cent of the senators who were not former governors opposed the amendment, 75 per cent of the former governors approved it. If the latter had divided their votes in the same way as their fellow senators did, the amendment would have been defeated by one vote rather than winning by seven.

The Brewster amendment represented an extreme victory for the states and the principle of shared functions. Later in the debate it was pointed out that some states had no airport programs or indeed no legislative authorization at all to concern themselves with airport development. A further amendment, passed without discussion and by voice vote, authorized the CAA to carry out airport projects directly with localities in those states which could not themselves participate for lack of the necessary legislation. The states could share in airport development, said the Senate, if they were in the least way prepared to do so. The choice was the states'. Only if they failed to provide

[8] In addition to the several resolutions of the Conference, telegrams from 46 governors endorsing channeling were read into the record.

enabling legislation for their own administrative agencies would the federal agency deal directly with local governments.

The House version of the bill was originally reported out by the Committee on Interstate and Foreign Commerce with no channeling provision whatsoever. It was amended on the floor with virtually no discussion and by voice vote to provide: "Nothing in this act shall authorize the submission of a project application by any municipality or other public agency which is subject to the law of any State if the submission of such project application by such municipality or other public agency is prohibited by the law of such State."[9] The bill was easily passed by the House in this form. The Conference Committee was presented in the two versions of the bill with what would seem to be a distinction without a difference. The Senate version provided for channeling of all funds through state agencies, but if states did not have appropriate agencies, then direct federal-local relationships were authorized. The House version said nothing about channeling, but any state by its own initiative could make channeling mandatory and thus prohibit direct federal-local negotiations. In both cases, the states clearly could control the administrative handling of the federal program. Nevertheless, the state governors and the former governors who were senators tried hard to have the Senate version of the bill adopted. Republican Senate members of the conference committee for a time held fast as a group. The conference committee remained deadlocked for four months. The bill finally reported and passed was substantially the House bill: affirmative state action was required if federal airport funds were to be channeled through state agencies.

The history of the 1946 National Airport bill is notable for the clear view it gives of the cross-cutting of party by other lines of influence. It is equally significant for the opposite views taken by the states, on the one hand, and the larger cities, on the other, in this case competing for participation in the sharing process. The role of the Congress was in many ways that of mediator, seeking in Senator McCarran's words "to effect a compromise"

[9] A subsequent attempt to require channeling was initially defeated, then passed by teller vote, and finally shelved by a roll call. The final defeat was a vote of 185–170, 164 Democrats and 20 Republicans opposing the mandatory channeling; 133 Republicans and 36 Democrats favoring it.

between state and local views.[10] The strength of the idea of shared functions was perhaps most marked in the unstated assumption by all concerned that the federal government would not do the airport construction job alone. Constitutional authority, fiscal predominance, administrative ease, and military necessity might have justified this course of action. There is no evidence to indicate that any responsible group or agency seriously considered it. The states did not get all they wanted in the bill. But their failure to achieve full victory carried no sting. The power to compel channeling—which was the power to insure their full sharing in the airport program—remained exclusively a state power.

The Social Security legislation of early New Deal days is a more important case illustrating the political process by which the states insure their basic sharing in national programs. The legislation may indeed have marked a turning point in the federal system. If the social security program had been established as an all-federal one, as it very nearly was, the American government might look very different today. In a revealing aside in the course of a book review, Rexford Guy Tugwell described how close he and Harry Hopkins came to establishing Social Security as a program administered completely by the national government:

> As an historical matter it was not hard to see that the states had declined in importance as responsibilities had gravitated to Washington. . . . And it was not a mistake to think that the states were obsolete and ought to be superseded by regions; the mistake was in thinking that it would be the policy of President Roosevelt to enhance the federal power (of which he was talking a good deal in those days of crisis) at the expense of that of the states. He seemed to conclude finally that both powers could be enhanced at the same time. . . . The evidence that he still clung to the Brandeis-Frankfurter view was not supplied until there occurred the intra-administration struggle within the Committee on Social Security. In this struggle Harry Hopkins and the writer [Tugwell] put up what seemed to them to be a

[10] U.S. Congress, Senate, Sub-Committee on Aviation of the Committee on Commerce, *Hearings, Federal Aid for Public Airports,* 79th Cong., 1st Sess. (March 13–23, 1945), p. 114.

sound argument against decentralization to the states. Miss Perkins' advisers were determined to use the social security system to bolster up the states. This appeared to be so costly an undertaking that it might jeopardize the system and, anyway, it would artificially interrupt the natural desuetude of the states. On an historic occasion Mr. Hopkins and the writer asked the President if it was wrong to go on objecting. The answer was not clear; but it was plain that the objections were not going to win his support. The objectors then withdrew from the committee and from then on neither had any contact with the formulation of the report, the shaping of the law, or its subsequent administration. Both regarded it as perhaps their worst defeat.[11]

There existed, as a matter of fact, several solid justifications for joint federal-state programs. The sharing-of-functions controversy raged most hotly over the administration of unemployment compensation. For one thing, the 1933 Wagner-Peyser Act had established employment offices on a federal-state basis (replacing an older all-federal program). This clearly "helped to fix the mold into which the unemployment insurance system was to be cast."[12] For another, a number of states already had operating systems of unemployment insurance and argued that a new federal-state program would be less damaging to ongoing activities than an all-federal one, especially since the systems were quite diverse. Wisconsin's system provided for compensation reserves on a plant or industrial basis, which probably would have been impossible to maintain under an all-national program, and a former Wisconsin official, Edwin E. Witte, was executive director of the Cabinet Committee on Economic Security which was drafting the new federal legislation. Third, it was believed that a federal-state system would have greater constitutional security than an all-federal one. Miss Perkins put great weight on this point.[13] Finally there were many arguments put forward with respect to the desirability of state experimentation, decentralization, and local participation.

[11] R. G. Tugwell and E. C. Banfield, "Grass Roots Democracy—Myth or Reality?" *Public Administration Review*, X (Winter, 1950), 48, 50.

[12] Paul Douglas, *Social Security in the United States* (New York: McGraw-Hill, 1936), p. 32.

[13] Frances Perkins, *The Roosevelt I Knew* (New York: Viking, 1946), p. 291.

None of these considerations or any combination of them was controlling. Mr. Tugwell is accurate in his recollection that the unemployment compensation program came very close to being established as an all-federal one. In addition to the general argument with respect to the "natural desuetude" of the states, there were good technical reasons for establishing an all-federal unemployment compensation program. The movement of workers and the consequences of unemployment were clearly national in scope, and a nationally uniform unemployment insurance scheme seemed highly desirable. Many relief and other depression programs had been administered directly from Washington. The states, administratively and financially, were in poor condition.

In the eyes of those directly concerned, the weight of the argument was in favor of the all-federal unemployment compensation program. Miss Perkins has revealed that the Cabinet Committee in fact made, relatively late in its deliberations, a formal decision to recommend such a program. But the decision was reversed in favor of the collaborative federal-state programs. The final decision was not made for technical reasons, but for political ones. Miss Perkins has written:

> After long discussion we [the Cabinet Committee] agreed to recommend a federal system [without state participation]. We went back and informed colleagues in our own Departments. Within the day I had telephone calls from members of the Committee saying that perhaps we had better meet again.
>
> There was grave doubt, our latest interviews with members of Congress had shown, that Congress would pass a law for a purely federal system. State jealousies and aspirations were involved. So we met again, and after three or four hours of debate we switched back to a federal-state system.[14]

The depression crisis, weighty technical considerations (although some technical advice was on the other side), the powerful influence of Tugwell, Hopkins, Wallace, and Morgenthau, the existence of overwhelming Democratic majorities in both

[14] *Ibid.*, pp. 291–92. Miss Perkins does not mention Tugwell's or Hopkins' views, but notes that Henry Wallace and Secretary of the Treasury Morgenthau argued for the all-federal system.

houses—all of these favorable factors were not sufficient to produce an all-federal unemployment compensation system. They were not sufficient because of decisive political considerations. The distribution of power within the majority party made an all-federal system impossible. Virtually the whole debate on the unemployment compensation bill, as introduced in its federal-state collaborative form, revolved around criticism of the power given to federal administrators. Amendments to the bill, proposed by Democrats and passed with Democratic votes, substantially curtailed even the limited power initially provided federal agencies. When the Cabinet Committee was making a following for its proposal and when the proposal itself was altered by the Congress, the localism of the legislator was the controlling factor. The lack of party solidarity produces through national legislation the marble cake of shared functions that characterizes the American federal system.

### LEGISLATIVE INVOLVEMENT IN THE ADMINISTRATIVE PROCESS[15]

The second manner in which undisciplined political parties establish the character of the American system is through the impact of congressmen and senators on national administrative agencies. The congressional interference is constant, effective, and institutionalized. It may be pegged on the broadest issues of national policy or on purely personal considerations, but it is most frequently exercised on behalf of local interests—individual, group, and governmental.

Some aspects of the process of legislative involvement in administrative affairs are formalized and well known. Administrative justifications before subcommittees on appropriations; the routine hearings before permanent legislative committees and subcommittees; and the work of special investigating or "watchdog" committees provide natural access points for members of the Congress to press constituency interests upon administrative officials. The Legislative Reorganization Act of 1946 made explicit the responsibility of the standing committees: each "shall exercise continuous watchfulness of the execution by the administrative agencies concerned of any laws, the subject matter of

[15] I am indebted to Kenneth E. Gray for aid on this section of the paper.

which is within the jurisdiction of such committee. . . ."[16] Both houses also have committees on Government Operations, each spawning a number of subcommittees. The House of Representatives has found the (Moss) Subcommittee on Government Information a tool for looking into all sorts of administrative processes on behalf of local constituents. The Congressional Committee on Printing has assumed a number of direct administrative responsibilities. Joint Committees of the Congress and the executive have for many years made decisions concerning the purchase of land for wild life refuges and national forests.[17] The General Accounting Office is a creature of Congress with important and pervasive executive functions.

The legislative involvement with executive business has been aided by a number of statutes in recent years that require administrators to report either past actions or future plans to Committees of Congress or to Congress as a whole. The 1955 Defense Appropriations bill, for example, required the Secretary of Defense to secure prior consent of the House and Senate Appropriations Committees before turning over departmental functions to private industry.[18] The Secretary of the Air Force, by a 1949 statute, was required to "come into agreement with" the House and Senate Armed Forces Committee before acquiring land for guided missile proving grounds.[19] Sometimes the statutes provide merely for "consultation" between congressional committees and administrative agencies; sometimes for reports; sometimes for a suspensive veto that Congress or one of its committees can exercise over administrative action.[20] An example of the last

[16] 79th Cong., 2d Sess., 60 *U.S. Stats.* I, 832.

[17] See Paul H. Appleby, *Policy and Administration* (University, Ala.: University of Alabama Press, 1949), pp. 8–10.

[18] Department of Defense Appropriations Act of July, 1955, Sec. 638. 69 *U.S. Stats.*, p. 321. The President strenuously opposed this provision, and it was eliminated in 1956.

[19] 63 *U.S. Stats.*, I, 66.

[20] Lease purchase agreements are subject to direct committee supervision. Public Law 519, 83d Cong., 2d Sess. (1954), amending the Public Buildings Act of 1949, reads (Title I, Sec. 411 (e) and Title II, Sec. 202 (g)) : "No appropriation shall be made for purchase contract projects which have not been approved by resolutions adopted by the Committee on Public Works of the Senate and House of Representatives respectively. . . ." Identical statements are included in legislation relating to the Post Office and General Service Administration. See the review of such statutes in J. Malcolm Smith

sort of control is provided by the Internal Revenue code which stipulates that the Commissioner of Internal Revenue may not make a tax refund or credit in excess of $200,000 until thirty days after he submits a report to the Joint Committee on Internal Revenue Taxation. The Joint Tax Committee maintains a "branch office" in the Bureau of Internal Revenue where members of the Committee's legal staff review administrative recommendations for tax refunds and credits and do not cavil at recommending that the legislative committee reverse administrative determinations.[21]

A general scrutiny of administrative stewardship is made possible by this elaborate formal network of legislative-administrative relationships. But the very nature of the reporting and consultation statutes, as well as the local propensities of the members of Congress, substantially turns the system into one in which, for better or worse, the legislator serves as the watchdog of national administrative actions on behalf of local constituents. The system formally provides for extensive joint responsibilities by congressional committees and administrative officers in the making of administrative decisions. Administrators in effect must "pre-clear" their actions with the appropriate subcommittee, in some cases with individual members. At the very least, an opportunity is provided congressmen and senators to register protests—in many cases having the effect of a veto—with respect to problems affecting their constituencies. At its worst, the system makes it possible for an individual member to bludgeon an entire department on behalf of local causes.

The formal and legally specified overviews of administrative action by legislative committees frequently encounter strenuous opposition by executive officers and are in some cases subject to

and Cornelius P. Cotter, "Administrative Accountability: Reporting to Congress," *Western Political Quarterly*, X (June, 1957), 405–15. Concurrent resolutions by Congress, as well as statutes, are used to terminate administrative powers, require administrative action, and veto administrative acts. See Cornelius P. Cotter and J. Malcolm Smith, "Administrative Accountability to Congress: the Concurrent Resolution," *Western Political Quarterly*, IX (December, 1956), 955–66. See also Kenneth T. Kofmehl, "Congressional Staffing: With Emphasis on the Professional Staff" (Ph.D. dissertation, Columbia University, 1956).

[21] See Sec. 3777 of the Internal Revenue code. In 1949–50, almost 1,000 cases involving $766 million were reviewed in this fashion.

constitutional objection. In any case, informal understandings are far more important than the provisions of law for producing continuous legislative involvement in administrative affairs. Rivers and Harbors legislation caricatures the process. Members of Congress nominally serve as officers of the leading interest group (the Rivers and Harbors Congress), and the Corps of Engineers has established procedures for entertaining local viewpoints in the field and for implementing them in Congress, subject only to whatever measures of control can be mustered by the Bureau of the Budget and the President. Institutional caricatures, like others, make overt what elsewhere may be hidden. Thus the Committee on Interstate and Foreign Commerce instructs the Department of Commerce and the regulatory agencies with respect to the imposition of licensing fees.[22] A House subcommittee prevents the Department of Defense from closing military hospitals that, according to defense officials, are no longer necessary.[23] The House Armed Services Committee, in an effort to keep military post exchanges from competing with local retailers, works out detailed, informal agreements with each of the services concerning what may and may not be sold at post exchanges. Regulations of the services implement these legislative-administrative settlements.[24] Appropriations hearings provide the stage for securing many commitments of this sort.

The most important and pervasive method of legislative participation in the administrative process is through activities of individual legislators on behalf of local constituents. Workers on the Hill call this their "case work." Alben Barkley had a story illustrating both the range of services rendered and the sometime ingratitude of the recipients:

> I called on a certain rural constituent and was shocked to hear him say he was thinking of voting for my opponent. I reminded him of the many things I had done for him as prosecuting attorney, as county judge, as congressman, and senator. I recalled how I had

[22] *Cong. Rec., Daily Digest,* 83d Cong., 2d Sess. (March 30, 1954), pp. 239–40.
[23] *Chicago Daily News,* May 3, 1957.
[24] Field notes, Washington, D.C., February 11, 1958. Consultation on what may be sold in commissary stores has a statutory base. See H.R. 12738, Sec. 613, Department of Defense Appropriations Bill, 85th Cong., 2d Sess.

helped get an access road built to his farm, how I had
visited him in a military hospital in France when he
was wounded in World War I, how I had assisted him
in securing his veteran's benefits, how I had arranged
his loan from the Farm Credit Administration, how I had
got him a disaster loan when the flood destroyed his
home, etc., etc.

"How can you think of voting for my opponent?" I
exhorted at the end of this long recital. "Surely you remember all these things I have done for you?"

"Yeah," he said, "I remember. But what in hell
have you done for me lately?"[25]

Barkley's joke is a form of caricature, and again it reveals
what is widespread but frequently unrecognized. The joke in
fact may be documented. Its exact counterpart is found in a
letter to a constituent written by Texas Congressman Wright
Patman. Mr. Patman was angry when he wrote his letter because
he had heard that the constituent was supporting another candidate for the Congressman's seat. The Congressman reviewed
his relationships with his constituent over a period of twenty
years. On no fewer than twenty occasions Mr. Patman had
interposed himself in administrative matters on behalf of this
single voter and his family. Ten of Mr. Patman's acts concerned
the Post Office Department (the Congressman not only secured
jobs for his constituent and members of his family, but saved
them from being dismissed when they misappropriated funds);
two concerned part-time jobs with the Bureau of the Census; one
involved an authorization of veterans' payments to students in a
school founded by his constituent; three concerned loans from
the Reconstruction Finance Corporation, the Small Defense
Plants Administration, and the Public Housing Administration;
and three concerned War Department matters involving the
names of ROTC officers who might make good candidates for
insurance sold by the Congressman's constituent.[26]

[25] From *That Reminds Me,* by Alben W. Barkley, p. 165. Copyright 1954
by Alben W. Barkley. Reprinted by permission of Doubleday & Company, Inc.

[26] The letter was placed on March 23, 1956, into the record of the Subcommittee for Special Investigations of the House Committee on Armed
Services investigating the sale of life insurance to prospective members of the
military service. It was reprinted in the *Reporter,* July 12, 1956, pp. 19–22.

The very tone of Mr. Patman's letter indicated his belief that all of this activity was perfectly normal and proper. He was doing what congressmen do naturally. Senator Lehman of New York spent considerable personal sums to augment his staff, the largest fraction of which devoted itself to constituent problems. Not that senatorial staffs are picayune. Senator Douglas revealed in 1957 that his offices in Washington and Chicago had twenty-one employees whose total salaries amounted to $119,222.[27] A good fraction of these people were involved in the simple process of opening the Senator's mail and finding an easy way of handling it—a form response, a stereotyped referral slip, or a request for a pamphlet from one of the departments. These processes involve little direct contact with the administration, though in more than a few instances the proper response, even if a canned one, is dependent upon a phone call to a bureau or a corridor conversation with a bureau representative.

Aside from clerical workers, Senator Douglas' personal staff in 1958 included three full-time persons in a Chicago office and five in Washington. Some of their work was concerned with publicity, party and campaign relations, and the Senator's obligations in legislation. But their principal task was to place problems of the Senator's constituents before the appropriate administrative offices in the way best calculated to achieve the constituents' satisfaction—and, it goes without saying, the constituents' votes for the Senator.[28]

[27] *Chicago Sun Times*, March 27, 1957, p. 10.
[28] The essential difference in the roles of American and English legislators is made clear when one compares their respective office staffs. Unless the M.P. holds a ministerial post, the government does not even provide him with an office. Since M.P.'s usually can't afford to pay for their own office accommodations in the neighborhood of the Parliament, most of them have no office at all. And the idea that twenty-one people at an expenditure of more than $100,000 a year would not be sufficient for an M.P. to do his job properly would only arouse the utmost mirth. Again, unless he holds an official post, the M.P. is not even supplied with a personal secretary from government funds. This does not mean that a British M.P. neglects to nurse his constituency. "Holding surgery" to listen to constituent complaints and proposals is a well-established part of a member's routine. But his course of action is not a demanding one with respect to the departments. Except for matters of information, the M.P. must take up his constituent problems with the ministers concerned, themselves controlled by party decisions, and on no significant issue may he transgress party policy or embarrass party steward-

The examples of Senators Lehman and Douglas are good ones because they should remove any doubts concerning the propriety of such acts of involvement by the legislator in administrative matters. In these matters, as in others, Messrs. Lehman and Douglas provide models of the ideal senator. There is no hint of venality or impropriety in these activities. They are a normal part of a senator's business. Senator Douglas' complaint is only that the government does not provide him with enough money to maintain an office staff large enough to do all the things he thinks ought to be done in response to the needs of his large constituency.

The looseness of the party system makes all of this activity possible. It also minimizes partisanship. Congressional and senatorial staff members form a pool of expertise, not least of all in casework problems, and a member of one party may have staff members of another. Congressional delegations often join forces without regard to party for city, state, or regional matters. For example, the California congressional group for a number of years has been formally organized for such purposes, and the entire West Coast delegation also works as a single unit in pursuit of regional interests. A senior congressman from a given state will often speak and act on behalf of the entire delegation. When it becomes known that a state's Republican senator is less efficient than his Democratic colleague in casework matters, Republican voters (including mayors and state legislators) find their way to the Democratic senator's office. They receive service all the more prompt and energetic because of the delight that the Democratic member and his staff have in building fences where none existed before. Even this minor partisan pinpricking may be absent. For example, Colorado Senators Millikin (Rep.) and Johnson (Dem.) maintained a common office, jointly staffed, to give service to those with general state problems. Correspondence from the office carried the signatures of both senators. This

---

ship or, as American legislators do as a matter of course, join with opposing members *contra* party *pro* locality. An opposition member has greater latitude, but still not that of successfully badgering bureaucrats up and down the line in behalf of local interests. If he tries this course of action, he is politely referred to the appropriate ministerial officer who, as a member of the majority party, has a powerful platform from which to respond.

co-operation continued for twelve years without a major disagreement.[29]

Although no exact calculation of the magnitude of the casework is possible, one can be sure it is very large indeed. The Office of Price Administration during the calendar year 1944 averaged 1,397 congressional "contacts" a week (phone calls, letters, and visits), an average of more than two for each five working days from each member of Congress. Peak periods were higher. In one twenty-week period of 1943, for example, congressional letters alone averaged 842 weekly.[30] Data for less vulnerable agencies during less intense periods are also available. In the ten working days between May 21 and June 4, 1958, the Department of the Interior received by actual count 553 pieces of congressional mail, plus an estimated 200 phone calls, an average of 75 congressional contacts per day.[31] The Office of Legislative Liaison of the Air Force averaged 3,000 "monitored" congressional contacts a month (as of the winter of 1958), and this did not count the personal contacts of the three Senate and four House liaison officers who were on full-time duty in the Capitol and House and Senate office buildings. (The Army, Navy, and Department of Defense each have separate liaison

[29] Field notes, February, 1958. The relationship was apparently a unique one. See *Roll Call* ("The Newspaper of Capitol Hill" published weekly by Capitol employees), February 12, 1958.

[30] Tabulated from "OPA and Congress," and "Report of Congressional Mail," Office of Price Administration, National Archives, Record Group 188. For technical reasons, all of these tabulations are underestimates. A report by an OPA official, Frank Ketcham, estimated (and probably overestimated) that from 1943 through 1946, the agency received 150,000 letters and telegrams and 300,000 telephone calls from members of Congress. See "Legislative Supervision of the Office of Price Administration" (typescript, 1947), National Archives, Office of Price Administration, Record Group 188.

OPA kept a separate record of *public* criticisms made of its operations by members of Congress. This recounts a lengthy list of bitter attacks in committee hearings, in public speeches, and on the floor of both houses. The March 1, 1944, entry is more meaningful than most others. It says simply: "No Congressional criticism this day." *OPA and Congress* (a duplicated intra-office information sheet), March 6, 1944.

[31] The count was of mail processed by the Correspondence Control Office in the Secretary's office. Many bureaus in the department, for example the highly decentralized Bureau of Land Management, undoubtedly handle congressional mail directly. The number given, therefore, is an underestimate. The phone calls are similarly underestimated.

staffs.) The congressional liaison office of the Department of Health, Education, and Welfare, according to an official estimate, responds to 500 congressional phone calls a month, and this, one can be sure, is only a fraction of the total number of calls to the many bureaus and field offices of the Department. An official tally by the Department of Agriculture recorded 5,564 letters from Congress during 35 working days, a daily average of 159.[32]

The administrative agencies seek to service congressional requests more effectively by establishing special liaison staffs and by institutionalizing procedures for congressional contacts. The Air Force in 1958 had, under the command of a major general, 137 people (55 officers and 82 civilians) working in its Office of Legislative Liaison.[33] Every congressional contact, except those made directly by Air Force officers who worked in the House and Senate office buildings, was "controlled" (the word was used to indicate the desire to render more rapid service), nine copies of a route slip being distributed strategically to the personnel concerned. Many agencies have rules that require congressional requests to be answered within a limited time (24 or 36 hours), and many others require all but routine responses to carry the Secretary's signature.

A similar institutionalization occurs within the congressional offices. We have already noted the specialization of function within the staffs. In addition, a given staff develops systems

---

[32] U.S. Congress, House, Subcommittee of the Committee on Appropriations, *Hearings, Department of Agriculture Appropriations for 1959,* 85th Cong., 2d Sess. (1958), p. 865. Magnitudes of interference are also impressive when measured from the side of the individual congressman or senator. In a single week, for example, one mid-western senator received 122 constituent letters which required 100 separate contacts with administrative agencies, involving 30 different bureaus or offices in twelve departments as well as twelve additional federal agencies. Kenneth E. Gray will further analyze these data in later reports. See his unpublished paper presented at the 1962 meeting of the American Political Science Association, "Congressional Interference in Administration."

[33] Field notes, January, 1958. For analysis of Liaison Offices, their numbers, functions and costs, see U.S. Congress, House, Committee on Government Operations, H.R. No. 2947, *Availability of Information from Federal Departments and Agencies,* 84th Cong., 2d Sess. (1956). For questionnaire and responses, see U.S. Congress, House, Committee on Government Operations, *Replies from Federal Agencies to Questionnaire Submitted by the Special Subcommittee on Government Information of the Committee on Government Operations,* 84th Cong., 1st Sess. (1955).

of priorities in handling cases; there are so many that all cannot be given an equal amount of time. Priority ratings are influenced by the source of the request (an old friend, a heavy campaign contributor, or a city mayor get special attention), but they are sufficiently flexible to bring out full effort when a "good case"—in terms of injustices done, or publicity potential, or constituency reaction—comes from an unknown and uninfluential constituent. Priority values determine whether a request is handled with a perfunctory phone call or routine reference—"just to get it from our desk to theirs"[34]—or with a full-scale assault upon administrative offices. The latter may start with a staff assistant making a casual inquiry and end with the congressman or senator meeting personally with a cabinet secretary, or attacking an agency on the floor, or introducing a bill, or asking for a special investigation. The institutionalization of interference also includes establishment of standards for ignoring or rejecting some constituent requests, based upon considerations of decency and propriety, as well as for defining acceptable and unacceptable modes of dealing with administrative officers. Both sets of standards vary from member to member and from staff to staff. It is not difficult to find examples of the abusive congressman demanding, as the price of his support, that an inordinate fraction of funds for a particular agency be spent in his district, or that normal procedures for rotation of military assignments be abrogated for a son of his important constituent. (By the same token, there exist administrators who promote their bureau, their project, or themselves by encouraging congressmen to expect such special considerations.) More generally, congressional involvement is amiable. It is directed at producing rapid and full consideration for constituent and district interests. It expects im-

[34] Even with respect to the most perfunctory inquiries, a member of Congress usually wants it to appear to the constituent that a special and "justifiably privileged" service has been rendered, whether that is the case or not. Staff members and administrators play this game knowingly with each other. When a service is rendered to a constituent that an administrative agency was going to do in any case and it only appears that congressional interference had something to do with it, full credit is likely to be publicly accorded the congressman by all hands. Staff members call this a "fall in" case. A special kind of "fall in" case results from the practice of administrative agencies informing congressmen and senators in advance of the decisions to spend money or build public works in their areas, thus allowing the members of Congress to make the announcements in the local newspapers.

partial treatment without favoritism,[35] but it also demands special consideration for hardship cases and other special circumstances. It assumes an adversary quality only when the normal give and take between legislative requests and administrative adjustment breaks down.

The legislator's ability to command information from the administrative agency, on the one hand, and his access to press, television and radio, on the other, produce a double sanction. Administrators know that any failure to satisfy congressional requests may result not only in congressional penalties, ranging from criticism to new legislation, but also in adverse publicity. Both sorts of penalties are avoided whenever possible, although where congressional requests are immoderate, administrative officers have recourse to both legislative and public means of defense. The typical means of avoiding clashes and of promoting the continuous executive-legislative collaboration necessary for administrative action is through the mechanism of "pre-clearance." Pre-clearance works in both directions. Legislators informally work out in advance with administrators what they later formally request. More relevantly here, administrative officers clear contemplated actions in advance with strategic subcommittees and members of Congress. The clearance is sought not only for new legislative and budget requests but also for contemplated administrative actions. Important clearance activities of this sort are those that seek advance approval of the congressmen and senators who represent localities to be affected by what a national agency is planning to do. Mechanisms of clearance range from a phone call to a congressman to full-scale conferences between bureau chiefs and committee chairmen with staff members from both sides in attendance. The informal periodic reporting of agencies to subcommittees is a particularly effective means of pre-clearing administrative acts.

The widespread and in many ways unpredictable character of legislative interference in administrative affairs has many consequences for the tone and character of American administrative behavior. From the perspective of this paper, the important consequence is the comprehensive, day-to-day—even hour-

---

[35] All congressional inquiries lead to two forms of favoritism. They hasten the consideration of the particular problem raised; and they move the decision from lower to higher levels of the administrative hierarchy.

by-hour—impact of local and state views on national programs. No point of substance or procedure is immune from congressional scrutiny. No point of access is neglected: from phone calls to regional offices to conferences with agency heads and the chief officers of the Bureau of the Budget; from cocktail conversations to full committee investigations. A very large portion of the entire weight of this impact is on behalf of individual constituents, group interests, and state and local governments. It is a weight that can alter procedures for screening immigration applications, divert the course of a national highway, change the tone of an international negotiation, and amend a social security or flood control law to accommodate local practices or fulfill local desires.

Virtually the whole process of legislative participation in administrative affairs would be impossible if the American party system were more tightly controlled from the top. With disciplined parties the free-wheeling interference of individual members on behalf of local constituents could not take place. It would not be tolerated. If members of the parties were responsive to their leadership, if they were committed to a program, if they were subject to discipline in the event of defection from that program, the administration of policy would be unified and controlled. The individual legislator would have less access to the administrator and less influence in altering administrative direction in terms of nonparty interests. To a corresponding degree there would be diminished the leavening of national administrative programs by state, local, and other group interests, interests that are so energetically represented by members of the Congress.[36]

[36] The discovery that pressure groups in Great Britain are vastly influential does not in any way alter this point. Indeed, it strengthens it. As Samuel H. Beer has pointed out, the relationships between interest groups and government in Britain are "quasi-corporative." The "individual legislator, and the legislature generally, under cabinet government occupy a less important position." The American legislative committees have no British counterparts. Interest groups in Britain are agglomerated in large associations, and they must focus on winning the support of the Minister and Chancellor of the Exchequer. In the United States there are more points at which pressure can and must be applied. Party control means precisely that pressure upon government can be effective only if approved by the party. Pressure groups therefore work in areas where party discipline is not exercised and, more importantly, in areas where their scope of effectiveness is defined by

## Morton Grodzins

THE ADMINISTRATOR AS POLITICIAN

Bluntly put, it can be said that the inability of national political leaders to control the legislative members of the party accounts, *ipso facto,* for their inability to control the national administration. Stated positively, the undisciplined party system compels administrators to seek political support for their programs. The parties do not supply this support, and administrators and their programs cannot survive without it. This leads to the third important manner in which the parties affect the operation of the American system: they make the administrator play a political role.

The previous discussion makes clear why some administrative officers walk in fear of the telephone. A bureau chief in the Department of Interior once told an interviewer that half of his fellow chiefs prayed each morning: "Oh Lord, let not the chairman of my appropriations subcommittee call me this day." But if a bureau chief is craven before a congressman, how then can he follow the directives of his own administrative superior? If a legislator can substantially interfere with the operation of an administrative office, how can a group of administrative offices concert their efforts into a unified program?

Administrators need not be craven. Some welcome conflict with congressmen; some are polite but unresponsive, and some just plain hide; some can find protection by appealing to other legislators; some serve other masters who themselves may be influential with significant congressional blocs; some are successful in protecting their own view and their agency program by deftly juggling the opposing views of congressmen, constituent groups, administrative superiors, and others concerned. The very multiplicity of pressures upon administrators provides opportunities for discretion, independence, and invention.

party and party-leader decisions. The American contrast—where, in Beer's words, "pressure politics is so much noisier and less tidy"—rests upon the lack of party control. See Beer's two excellent articles, "Pressure Groups and Parties in Britain" and "The Representation of Interests in British Government," *American Political Science Review,* L (March, 1956) , 1–23; LI (September, 1957) , 613–50. Also W. J. M. MacKenzie, "Pressure Groups in British Government: Historical Background," *British Journal of Sociology,* VI (June, 1955) , 133–48; S. E. Finer, *Anonymous Empire* (London: Pall Mall Press, 1958) ; J. D. Stewart, *British Pressure Groups* (Oxford: Clarendon Press, 1958) .

These activities of the administrator do not sound significantly different from the activities of many congressmen. And they are not. The higher administrator, as Paul Appleby and others have made clear, performs an intrinsically political role.[37] The reason such a role is possible for the administrator is the same reason that accounts for the interference in administration on the part of the legislator. The administrator can play politician, just as the politician can play administrator, because the parties are without program and without discipline.

The administrator's response to the unprotected position in which the party situation places him is a natural one: he seeks support where he can find it. One ever-present task is that of nursing the Congress of the United States, the crucial constituency which ultimately controls his agency's budget and program. For this task he may partially depend on the clients his agency serves. To take an easy example, the Veterans' Administration can rely to some degree upon veterans' organizations to reward congressional supporters and punish congressional opponents of V.A. programs. But this is neither a quick nor a certain process. And it is necessary for the administrator to lubricate the continuous interaction his agency has with the Congress and individual congressman by a sympathetic consideration of, if not downright accommodation to, congressional requests. This is the administrative basis of the successful congressional case work we have already considered. An additional point can now be made clear. The casework relationship works both ways. Not only is the congressman dependent upon administrative accommodation; a more fundamental truth is the administrator's dependence upon the congressman.

From the administrator's side, the servicing of congressional requests is to build the political support without which the administrative job could not continue. The servicing role sometimes takes an extreme form. "We try to consider ourselves part of the senators' staffs," an agency liaison officer recently told an interviewer. This posture is sometimes assumed to offset the less

[37] Paul Appleby, *op. cit.*, and *Big Democracy* (New York: Knopf, 1945); Norton E. Long, "Power and Administration," *Public Administration Review*, IX (Autumn, 1949), 257–64; Herbert A. Simon, Donald W. Smithburg, and Victor A. Thompson, *Public Administration* (New York: Knopf, 1950), pp. 381–401; Harlan Cleveland, "The Executive and the Public Interest," *Annals*, CCCVII (September, 1956), 37–54.

accommodating attitudes of bureau workers who view congressional interference with something less than receptivity. But even the completely task-oriented administrator must be sensitive to the relationship between casework requests, on the one side, and budgetary and legislative support, on the other. "You do a good job handling the personal problems and requests of a Congressman," a White House officer said, "and you have an easier time convincing him to back your program."[38] Thus there is an important linkage between the nursing of congressional requests on local matters and the most comprehensive national programs. The administrator must accommodate to the former as a means of gaining support for the latter. Other considerations of course affect congressional support of administrative programs. But the importance of administrative service to members of Congress is evident at every hand, particularly in the size and cost of the liaison staffs themselves. At least five staffs—Army, Navy, Air Force, Veterans' Administration, and Civil Service Commission—maintain quick-service offices on Capitol Hill. Other liaison officers headquarter themselves in the offices of friendly congressmen or senators. Liaison with the highest executive officers is close and continuous. "Pre-clearance" of administrative acts works at every level, a cabinet officer consulting a subcommittee chairman on important points, a liaison clerk calling a freshman congressman on others.

The need for executive offices to build their own political support is the principal cause of that conflict which characterizes American administrative life—among departments and among bureaus within departments. It accounts for the relative immunity of some agencies from presidential control; and the stronger the source of independent support, the more immune the agency is. It explains why an act of legislation may not at all define the real power of an administrative office.[39] The necessity put upon administrators to build political support also provides the sociological base for Charles G. Dawes' otherwise enigmatic

[38] Quoted in *Wall Street Journal*, June 16, 1959.

[39] "A price control law wrung from a reluctant Congress by an amorphous and unstable combination of consumer and labor groups is formally the same as a law enacting a support price program for agriculture backed by the disciplined organizations of farmers and their congressmen. [But] the differences for the scope and effectiveness of administration are obvious." Long, *loc. cit.*, p. 257.

statement that "every member of the Cabinet is the natural enemy of the President."[40]

One result of administrative politics is that the administrative agency may become the captive of the nationwide interest groups it serves or presumably regulates. In such cases no government may come out with effective authority: the winners are the interest groups themselves. But in a very large number of cases, states and localities are also influence winners. The position of states and localities may be directly tied to nationwide interest groups: the United States Conference of Mayors has been at one with the Congress of Industrial Organizations, for example, in urging federal urban renewal programs. In other cases, the state or local views (frequently opposed to each other) may be represented on their own: as when a congressman hastens the transfer of a defense airport to a municipality, or a group of congressmen aids state welfare officers in bringing about changes in federal public assistance rules, or a bureau chief, under pressure from city lobbyists and the state delegation (one of whom is a key figure in the bureau's appropriations subcommittee), orders the establishment of a field office where it otherwise would not have been.[41] The complete mobilization of a state or locality produces maximum potency. A group of state legislators and administrators will travel to Washington with the governor's blessing, accompanied by leading businessmen and several administrative specialists from state offices. They will convene a meeting which is attended by both of the state's senators and a majority of the state's congressmen. The federal administrators summoned to such a meeting perforce pay careful heed to the requests of the group.

Bureaucrats and the bureaucratic system in the United States do not at all follow the model classically set forth by Max

<hr/>

[40] I am indebted to Louis Brownlow for the Dawes quotation. Richard F. Fenno, Jr., supplies an overview of the literature on presidential-cabinet relationships and an illuminating case study of the divisive effects of independent sources of support in "President-Cabinet Relations: A Pattern and a Case Study," *American Political Science Review*, LII (June, 1958), 388–405.

[41] Local officers even attempt to use this route of influence to alter *state* policies. See the testimony of Mayor Richardson Dilworth of Philadelphia before the (Fountain) Subcommittee of the Committee on Government Operations, House of Representatives, 85th Cong., 1st Sess., *Hearings*, Part I, pp. 357–58.

Weber. The system is not described by his term "monocratic control," control by one from the top. Such control must be predicated upon the existence of a program—defined, administered, and policed by an organized majority. The United States congressional majority is relatively unorganized. It has no single program, no single leader, no effective means for political punishment, and therefore no easy mechanism for controlling the political activity of the bureaucrat. Lack of political program and control compels political activity on the part of the administrator. Without this activity he runs the risk of having no program to administer. The total impact of the political role of the bureaucrat is not unmixed. He may use his political power to aggrandize his own position and his own agency, thus shifting the power focus to the center. He may produce, or be forced into, a situation in which no government is in effective control. But always he must find support from legislators tied closely to state and local constituencies and state and local governments. The political activity of the administrator, like the administrative activity of the legislator, must often be turned to representing state and local interests in national programs.

THE MULTIPLE CRACK

Those who have discovered the politics of the administrator have not made sufficiently clear that his political attributes are not unique. His role in politics is matched by that of other individual citizens and other professional and vocational groups. The administrator is in a somewhat privileged position, but it differs in degree, not in kind.

This suggests a fourth manner in which parties crucially affect the operation of the American system. Weber predicted that "the living machine which is bureaucracy, in co-operation with the inorganic-physical-machine, is bringing about the structure of super- and sub-ordination which will characterize the future. In that structure human beings will be forced into impotent obedience—like fellaheen in the ancient Egyptian state." What a misreading of the current American situation this is. The picture is not one of obedience. It is one in which individuals and groups attempt to influence governmental policy at every step of the legislative-administrative process.

We call this the "multiple crack" attribute of American

government. "Crack" has two meanings. It means fissure, a place for individuals and groups to make their views known; in this meaning crack is almost synonymous with what the literature discusses as "access."[42] But access alone is too static a concept. Crack also means a wallop, a smack at government in an attempt to influence policy.

If the parties were more disciplined, the result would of course not be a cessation of the process by which individuals and groups impinge themselves upon the central government. But the present state of the American parties clearly allows for a far greater operation of the multiple crack than would be possible under the conditions of centralized party control. Local and other interests make themselves felt in the British system. But it would be difficult to adduce any case in which British interests act as American ones characteristically do: finding and attempting to exploit cracks at literally uncountable points in the legislative-administrative process. If legislative lobbying (from the committee stages to the conference committee) does not produce results, those seeking action meet with the cabinet secretary. His immediate associates are petitioned. Bureau chiefs and their aides are hit. Field officers are put under pressure. Campaigns are instituted by which friends of the agency apply a secondary influence on behalf of the interested party. A conference with the President may be urged. Attempts may be made to activate the wife of the President or other members of his immediate family.

To these multiple points for bringing influence must be added the multiple voices of the influencers. Consider, for example, those in a small town who wish to have a federal action taken, whether it be to amend a flood control law, or to secure a sewage disposal grant, or to have a surplus plant sold to a local businessman. The easy merging of public and private interests[43] at the local level means that at selected points in the decision-

[42] Pendleton Herring, *The Politics of Democracy* (New York: Norton, 1940), p. 431; David B. Truman, *The Governmental Process* (New York: Knopf, 1951), pp. 507–8.
[43] The mixture of the public and private in American governmental affairs will be the subject of later publications by the University of Chicago federalism workshop. See Morton Grodzins, "Local Strength in the American Federal System: The Mobilization of Public-Private Influence," in Marian D. Irish (ed.), *Continuing Crisis in American Politics* (Englewood Cliffs, N.J.: Prentice-Hall, Inc., 1963), pp. 132–54.

making chain the local Chamber of Commerce speaks; at other points it is the Rotary Club; at others the mayor or city manager, and at still others an engineering consultant or fiscal specialist. In many matters the state or national professional organizations of local officials can be enlisted. In almost every case individual congressmen and senators, and not infrequently whole state delegations, will make the local cause their own. Federal field officers who service localities not infrequently assume local views. So may elected and appointed state officers. Friendships are exploited, and political mortgages called due. The voices are many, but the cause is one. Many people and groups may accumulate pressures at a single point, and, according to rough criteria of efficiency, forces are allocated where they will do the most good. If a phone call to a congressman is deemed helpful, it will be made by a person or group close to the congressman. If a conference in a senator's office will expedite matters, someone on the local scene can be found to make such a conference possible and effective. If technical information is needed, technicians will supply it.

All local causes, of course, need not be so energetically or efficiently pursued, and even if the need exists the skill and energy may not. The competition of interests—within single localities, between them, between localities and other interests, and between localities and states—complicates the process. Acceptance of a given locality's view may be dependent upon the defeat, but more typically it rests upon the ignorance or acquiescence, of other interested groups. Despite all qualifications, two facts are indisputable. The lack of central discipline within the party system makes the multiple crack possible and profitable for those who exploit it. The effect of the multiple crack is further to disperse decision-making power within the institutions of the central government and between the central and peripheral governments.

### III. Conclusion

Physicists have postulated the existence of subatomic antiparticles that exhibit characteristics opposite to those of particles. One is tempted to say that it would be appropriate to consider American political parties as antiparties. The classical party functions are functions of gathering together segments of power and wielding them as one. The American parties, as we have seen, do the opposite: they characteristically serve to disperse power. In this sense they are antiparties, not parties. Many responsible voices have urged that it would be in the national interest if the antiparties were transformed into parties, that is, given programs and discipline and the sort of leadership that would elevate centrally determined values to positions of greater relative importance. This argument is honorable with age; it was first made in 1879 by Woodrow Wilson.[44] The argument is based, as Austin Ranney has pointed out, on a commitment to unlimited majority rule (rather than the preservation of minority rights against majority rule), and on defects in governing that are judged to be the consequence of existing decentralized parties. One such defect is alleged to be the difficulty of setting a general course of policy for the government as a whole. A related defect is that special interests gain undeserved governmental privileges. A third is that disunited parties deprive voters of clear choices and make it impossible to tell who is responsible for particular acts of government. Still a fourth alleged deficiency is that the parochialism of party members makes parties "meaningless and even dishonest in the mind of the public."[45]

It is remarkable how many of those who believe in the desirability of disciplined parties see trends and social forces moving in that direction, while those who believe not, see not.[46] There is no room in this paper for a detailed analysis of the evidence brought forward in support of the thesis that parties

[44] In a paper published while Wilson was still an undergraduate, and later elaborated by him in several major works. See Austin Ranney, *The Doctrine of Responsible Party Government* (Urbana: University of Illinois Press, 1954), p. 25.

[45] See a Report of the Committee on Political Parties of the American Political Science Association, "Toward a More Responsible Two-Party System," published as a supplement to *The American Political Science Review*, XLIV (September, 1950). The quotation is from James MacGregor Burns, *Congress on Trial* (New York: Harper, 1949), p. 46. See also E. E. Schattschneider, *Party Government* (New York: Rinehart, 1942).

[46] See the several works by E. E. Schattschneider, and notably, with respect to the emergence of national, disciplined parties, his "United States: The Functional Approach to Party Government," in Sigmund Neumann (ed.), *Modern Political Parties* (Chicago: University of Chicago Press, 1956), pp. 194–215; also Part III of the Report of the Committee on Political Parties of the American Political Science Association, cited above; Paul T. David, "The Changing Party Pattern," *Antioch Review*, XVI (Fall, 1956), 333–50.

are, in fact, becoming significantly more centralized, disciplined, and programmatic. In general, this evidence is not persuasive. It suffers from imprecision as to what is allegedly being demonstrated. For example, centralization in the management of presidential campaigns becomes confused with the far more important, central leadership over congressional votes, though the former assuredly can grow without concomitant growth of the latter. Some of the evidence brought forward to demonstrate party centralization is indisputable; for example, that party membership is important in determining how a member of Congress votes. But such evidence is partial and overshadowed by other facts: there are no data that show any tendency towards the *increasing* importance of the party label in determining congressional votes. And, in any case, hardly any national legislation, not even legislation strongly supported by a popular President whose party controls both houses, is passed by the votes of a single party; defectors from the other party are almost invariably needed to offset defections from the majority. Other evidence advanced to support the thesis of growing party centralization is more difficult to assess. For example, Paul T. David has suggested that "centralization is . . . a product of the cohesion that is induced by competition."[47] He is here pointing to consequences that he sees in the disappearance of one-party states. There is some evidence that congressmen who win in close elections are indeed more likely to agree with congressional leaders than are those from safe constituencies. But this relationship has been shown to be true *only* for Democrats when there was a Democratic President, and even then it does not hold for Southern Democrats.[48] Fewer safe Democratic seats in the South might, in fact, produce fewer congressmen who buck the leader-

[47] Paul T. David, "The Changing Political Parties," in Marian D. Irish (ed.), *op. cit.*, p. 54.

[48] David B. Truman, *The Congressional Party* (New York: John Wiley, 1959), pp. 212 ff. Duncan MacRae, Jr., who studied the same Congress, shows that Republicans who won by narrow margins were more likely to be sensitive to constituency than those winning by wide margins, but that this relationship was not true for Democrats. (*Dimensions of Congressional Voting* [Berkeley: University of California Press, 1958], pp. 294–98.) The Truman and MacRae evidence together suggests that the election-margin data must be qualified by data on presidential leadership before they are useful for predicting adherence to party leadership.

ship as a matter of course. On the other hand, the consequence might simply be the further distribution of mavericks among *both* parties, it being plausible that a Southern victor might retain his Southernness whether elected under a Democratic or a Republican label. Without further evidence, which can come only with the passage of time, it is not possible to say what effect increased party competition in the South will have on congressional willingness to follow party leaders.

If it is true that the form and style of political parties reflect both constitutional arrangements and social structure, then it follows that a basic alteration in parties—their centralization—must be preceded by basic changes in constitutional practice and in the parties' social base. One would expect the constitutional changes to include some central control over congressional nominations, a decline in the importance of the Senate, and a desuetude in the functions of the Supreme Court. These are changes in constitutional practice which conceivably might not need formal constitutional amendment. Beyond them lie needed formal amendments, such as the one that would provide for the simultaneous election of the President and the Congress. As for required social changes, an intellectual commitment to unlimited majority rule is less important than the conviction by large population groups that their basic situation would be improved by centralized and programmatic parties, a development that probably depends upon growing class-consciousness, greater regional differences, or other marks of divisiveness which efface the tendency of extensive republics, in Madison's words, "to break and control the violence of faction." If the turn towards party centralization takes place, it is not likely that theoreticians will have to debate the meaning of what is happening: the needed constitutional and social changes are so fundamental that, if they do occur, they will be unmistakable.

A political system cannot be designed to serve antithetical ends, and every system suffers the ills of its own virtues. We have seen that American political parties operate to maintain a division of strength between the central government and the geographical (and other) peripheries. This division of strength has many values; not the least of them are the widespread generation of energies and allocation of responsibilities, and the defenses erected against authoritarian rule. The defects of the system include, most importantly, the nation's sometime slowness in responding to national leadership in a period of crisis, especially when crisis is confused with the norm. It is difficult to cure the defect without debasing the virtue. Tightening party control at the top decreases strength at the base. Centralized parties would seriously attenuate the four characteristics of the American system discussed above. If control from the top were *strictly* applied, the characteristics might entirely disappear. To be specific, if disciplined and programmatic parties were achieved:

1. It would make far less likely legislation that takes heavily into account the desires and prejudices of the highly decentralized power groups and institutions of the country, including the state and local governments.

2. It would to a large extent prevent national legislators, individually and collectively, from intruding themselves on behalf of non-national interests in national administrative programs.

3. It would deprive administrative officers of a large part of their political weight, a weight often used to foster state, local, and other powers.

4. It would dampen the process by which individuals and groups, including state and local political leaders, take multiple cracks at the national government in order to steer legislation and administration in ways congenial to them and the institutions they represent.

The sharing of functions is, in fact, the sharing of power. This sharing is the hallmark of modern American federalism. To it can be traced in large part the continued important participation of state and localities in virtually all programs of government: the marble cake of administration. It accounts, with historical consideration added, for the fact that federal and state laws share, rather than exclusively occupy, areas of service and regulation. It provides the basis for states and localities to exercise an extraordinarily wide range of informal influence over federal legislation and administrative programs, an influence that is sometimes channeled through members of Congress but which is also manifest through the activities of professional organizations and direct "cracks" at federal agencies by state and local officers. It indicates, in sum, the existence of a substantial devolution of power in the American political system.

# Herbert J. Storing

•

# POLITICAL PARTIES AND
# THE BUREAUCRACY

1

Following a conference at Morningside Heights in September, 1952, Senator Robert Taft announced that the Republican candidate for the Presidency, General Eisenhower, had "stated without qualification that in the making of appointments at high levels or low levels there will be no discrimination against anyone because he or she has supported me, and that he is determined to maintain the unity of the entire party by taking counsel with all factions and points of view."[1] Thus in the event of a Republican victory, the Taft supporters were to be given a share in the formulation and administration of government policy; and government offices, high and low, were not to be distributed in such a way as to punish the Taft group or to weaken its influence within the Republican Party. This was one of the few relatively specific terms of the famous accommodation at Morningside Heights, and it illustrates the persistent and well-known concern of American political parties with government offices. Traditionally the parties have depended upon public offices to sustain themselves as organizations and to give effect to their policies; the civil service is both the trough at which they feed and the instrument by which they govern. In this paper we shall be concerned primarily with the latter part of the relationship.[2]

If the Eisenhower-Taft agreement illustrates the continued

[1] *New York Times*, September 13, p. 6.

[2] For a valuable discussion emphasizing questions arising out of the traditional organizational dependence of parties on patronage, see Harvey C. Mansfield, "Political Parties, Patronage, and the Federal Government Service," *The Federal Government Service* (New York: The American Assembly, Columbia University, 1954), pp. 81–112.

concern of political parties with public offices, the experience of the Eisenhower administration with patronage illustrates (among other things) the extent to which the political party today is limited in its direct access to federal offices for any purpose. In 1952 about 85 per cent of the federal service was under the merit system, and much of the remainder was practically unavailable for party purposes, either because the incumbents were needed or because the jobs were, for one reason or another, unattractive. Although the Republicans were accused of raiding the merit system in search of spoils, the steps taken to provide more places for Republicans were in fact very limited. By 1954 the proportion of the service under the merit system had dropped by only 2 or 3 per cent. There was, it is true, a certain amount of party "clearance" even for positions filled by examination, but as one historian of the civil service has said, "The pickings for the National Committee have . . . been the leanest in history."[3] There is still some patronage available to the political party, especially at the beginning of a new administration, and the old tree will still produce an occasional plum (such as the 73 federal judgeships created in 1961) ; but the trend in the direction of the merit system is not likely to be reversed.

This exclusion of the political party from the vast majority of federal offices has not, of course, come about by accident or thoughtless adaptation to changed circumstances. It resulted from a deliberate reform of the American political system which found expression primarily in the Pendleton Act of 1883. As is well known, this Act established a bipartisan Civil Service Commission charged, among other things, to provide open competitive examinations for entry into the "classified" federal service. Originally only about 10 per cent of the 140,000 positions in the federal service were covered, but provision was made for extensions by executive order. Except for the provision that no person should be removed for failure to contribute time or money to a political party, the Act imposed no limitations on removal from office; but limitations were imposed later, especially with respect to veterans. Later legislation also sought to complete the "neutralization" of the public administration by severely limiting the political activities of civil servants.

[3] Paul P. Van Riper, *History of the United States Civil Service* (Evanston, Ill.: Row, Peterson and Co., 1958) , p. 491.

## Political Parties and the Bureaucracy

The post-Civil War reform movement which led to this legislation was directed immediately at the civil service, but its more fundamental objective was the reform of political parties. While the reformers did not seek to eradicate parties, they were, like the American Founders, keenly aware that "party spirit, from the first, has been the terror of republics."[4] It is, George Curtis said, "the one fire that needs no fanning. The first duty of patriotism is to keep that fire low."[5] Specifically, the reformers were trying to rid the country of the spoils system, in which they saw three evils:

1. By distributing public office as the booty of party warfare, the spoils system introduced gross inefficiency and corruption into the public administration.

2. By basing political parties on a network of selfish private relationships, the spoils system distorted and frustrated the expression of the popular will.

3. By channelling men's minds along the lines of private and narrow group interest and away from a concern with the public interest, the spoils system corrupted American political life and character.

Unlike their successors, the early reformers—such men as George Curtis, Dorman Eaton, and Carl Schurz—thought that administrative inefficiency was the least of these evils. "[T]he question whether the Departments at Washington are managed well or badly," said Carl Schurz, "is, in proportion to the whole problem, an insignificant question after all. . . . The most important point to my mind is, how we can remove that element of demoralization which the now prevailing mode of distributing office has introduced into the body-politic."[6] Similarly Dorman Eaton wrote that "civil service reform is not merely a mode of procedure and an economy, but has become a vital question of principle and public morality, involving the counterpoise and in no small degree the stability of the government itself."[7] In an

[4] The Relation Between Morals and Politics," in *Orations and Addresses of George William Curtis*, ed. Charles E. Norton (New York: Harper & Brothers, 1894) , II, 124.

[5] "The Reason and the Result of Civil Service Reform," *ibid.*, II, 387.

[6] Speech in the Senate, January 27, 1871, in *Speeches, Correspondence and Political Papers of Carl Schurz*, ed. Frederic Bancroft (New York: G. P. Putnam's Sons, 1913) , II, 123.

[7] *Civil Service in Great Britain* (New York: Harper & Brothers, 1880) , p. 438.

important statement of the object of civil service reform in an editorial for *Harper's Weekly* Schurz conceded that one aim was "an improved conduct of the public business."

> But the ultimate end of civil service reform is something far more important than a mere improvement in the machinery of administration. It is to elevate the character of our political life by eliminating from it as much as possible the demoralizing elements of favoritism and of mercenary motives which under the spoils system have become the moving powers in our politics. It is to rescue our political parties, and in a great measure the management of our public affairs, from the control of men whose whole statesmanship consists in the low arts of office-mongering, and many of whom would never have risen to power had not the spoils system furnished them the means and opportunities for organizing gangs of political followers as mercenary as themselves. It is to restore ability, high character, and true public spirit once more to their legitimate spheres in our public life, and to make active politics once more attractive to men of self-respect and high patriotic aspirations.[8]

Many of the reformers were Abolitionists in the controversy over slavery and regarded civil service reform as an extension of the same movement. Having freed the Negro slaves, they argued, it was time to free the civil service from its slavery to political parties. Like the system of chattel slavery, the spoils system corrupts slave, master, and the community that gives it countenance. The reformers' righteous indignation was founded on their conviction that the only two political questions of their time about which reasonable and patriotic men could not differ were Negro slavery and civil service reform. "Since the movement against personal slavery there has been nothing more truly American than this absolutely unselfish and patriotic demand for the emancipation of the Civil Service."[9] In conse-

---

[8] XXXVII (July 1, 1893), 614.

[9] "The Administration and Reform," in *Orations and Addresses of George William Curtis*, II, 359. Another reformer asserted, "no other public issue since the agitation against slavery has been so clearly and incontestably proved as Civil Service Reform. Every other question has two sides and a conclusion must be formed by balancing the advantages and disadvantages of each. . . . But the necessity of abolishing the evils which have accompanied the spoils system seems so clear and the methods proposed so perfectly

quence of their abundant and rather rigid morality, the civil service reformers were often scorned as idealistic dreamers, blind to the realities of American politics. But they did more than preach that good government is good. They had a specific, hard-headed program by means of which they proposed to purify American parties and elevate American politics.

This program and the reasoning on which it was based were given remarkably clear expression by William Dudley Foulke, who was active in the reform movement both nationally and in his own state of Indiana. Foulke explained that there are three major remedies that can be applied to corruption: penal legislation, which is necessary but effective only for the graver crimes; appeal to the moral sense of the community, which is desirable but often ineffective; and removal of the temptation, which is the principle of civil service reform.

> The great purpose of [civil service reform] is not so much to provide an efficient civil service (although it does this) as to remove the temptation to use the offices of the government for personal or party ends, in other words, to remove the incentive to that kind of political corruption which is nourished by the hope of office. It does this by something akin to a mechanical contrivance, making it automatically impossible for the politician seeking the control of patronage to appoint the particular man he wants. It was the concurrence of personal discretion with party government which brought in the spoils system, and rules requiring appointments by competitive examinations destroy this personal discretion.[10]

Thus while the problem was fundamentally a moral and political one, the solution was found in "something akin to a mechanical contrivance." Without attempting to plumb philosophical depths, the reformers reasoned that the immediate cause of political corruption was the spoils system; the spoils system, in turn, depended upon the discretion of appointing officers in choosing their subordinates. Abolish that discretion and you abolish the spoils system and the corruption flowing from it.

---

adapted to the purpose that I find it hard to understand how any unprejudiced mind, after careful study of the subject, can oppose the competitive system." William Dudley Foulke, *Fighting the Spoilsmen* (New York: G. P. Putnam's Sons, 1919), p. 3. Copyright 1919 by G. P. Putnam's Sons.

[10] *Ibid.*, pp. 9–10.

Although this chain of reasoning is not simply wrong, it is certainly insufficient. Civil service reform was not so efficacious as the reformers had expected in purifying politics and raising the moral tone of the community, and it brought new and unanticipated problems. Yet corruption *was* very considerably reduced, and politics *did* become less a matter of sheer self-seeking; most people would regard these as gains. One might imagine a moderate reformer asking us to imagine a situation where, not half, but all of the people were moved by nothing but selfish interests and where the political system positively fostered this tendency. Conceive the utter degradation and disaster to which such a system must inevitably lead. These are the results which, but for civil service reform, the spoils system might well have produced.

It is undeniable, however, that the reformers grossly oversimplified the problem of popular government. They were inclined to think that, once the spoils system was out of the way, citizens would become pure, leaders noble, and politics patriotic. "[B]y making election, not a fight for plunder, but a contest of principle," civil service reform would make "the honest will of the people the actual government of the country."[11] Although the reformers often described their movement as a return to the original principles of the American republic, they paid too little heed to the Founders' warning that a government fit for angels is not fit for men. Confronted with the need to rid American politics of selfishness run riot, they underestimated the enduring force of selfish interests, and consequently they failed to recognize sufficiently the permanent need to take account of such interests. They forgot the wisdom that lay in the Founders' "policy of supplying by opposite and rival interests, the defect of better motives. . . ." It is an indication of the extent to which the reformers' ideas still dominate our political thinking that we have to rediscover the lesson that political stability may be found in a politics of interests. And it is ironical that this primary principle of the first American planners and reformers, the Founding Fathers, should now appear in the guise of an argument against planning and reform.

[11] "The Administration and Reform," in *Orations and Addresses of George William Curtis*, II, 359.

## Political Parties and the Bureaucracy

2

With the passage of the Pendleton Act and the steady extension of the merit system in the federal service, the immediate objectives of the reformers were largely accomplishd. Although the question of civil service reform erupted periodically, it ceased to be a major political issue. The reform movement did not die, but it moved from the political arena to the universities. The men associated with the second phase of reform were not primarily agitators, pamphleteers, and politicians, like Schurz and Curtis, but university professors, like Frank Goodnow, or professor-politicians, like Woodrow Wilson.

This second generation of reformer–political scientists sought to state systematically the theory of government implicit in the reform movement and to elaborate in more detail its practical consequences. In so doing they established the main lines from which most contemporary thinking about political parties and public administration derives. The key words are "responsible parties" and "efficient administration." As these men generally saw it, the ideal democracy consists, as it were, of two pyramids joined at the top. The will of the people flows up through the pyramid of politics where it is collected by political parties and formed into programs of legislation. The programs of the majority party then flow down through the administrative pyramid where they are implemented in the most efficient manner. According to this theory the prime requisites of a civil service are political neutrality and technical competence. The civil servant is not supposed to make policy. He decides, according to scientifically established technical criteria, the best, that is, most efficient, way to accomplish any given ends. Those ends are set by his political superiors who are responsible through the party to the people.

In spite of some fairly obvious difficulties, this theory proved to be extremely durable, because it seems to state simply and clearly the whole problem of democratic government: to ensure the free expression and the efficient implementation of the popular will. With customary diligence and thoroughness the academicians set about investigating and explaining how the pyramid of politics and the pyramid of administration ought to be governed, each according to its proper principle. Proposals for the reform of political parties as such are dealt with in other papers in this series, but it is significant that these proposals have fared much worse than proposals for the reform of administration. Thus while the report of the American Political Science Association on *A More Responsible Two-Party System* has produced little but mild academic controversy, its predecessor and intellectual companion, the 1937 report of the President's Committee on Administrative Management, was widely accepted and largely implemented. A new and vigorous discipline of administration has grown up within the universities, and it trains and fosters a huge corps of professional administrators. Public administration today is subjected to continuous and exhaustive analysis, and a stream of proposals for improvement flows out of universities, research bureaus, and government offices. Administrative theorists and practitioners seem to have moved steadily forward in their understanding, improvement, and conduct of public administration.

So successful is this movement that there has been a tendency to ignore the crucial question of the proper *connection* between administration and politics. The stock answer is that of course the political master gives the orders, but he should not meddle in the activities of his administrative servants; if he does he will only get in the way of the efficient implementation of his own orders. "Administrative questions are not political questions," Wilson said. "Although politics sets the tasks for administration, it should not be suffered to manipulate its offices."[12] It is true that even the most ardent proponents of a neutral civil service rarely went so far as to assert that the intermediate and lower levels of public administration could be altogether free of direct political influence. There were even some doubts whether political control at the top could ever be sufficient to keep the administration politically responsible; but generally students and reformers of administration were too busy extending the merit system, neutralizing the civil service, and devising principles of administration to concern themselves much with the "external" problem of political control. In any case, the logic of the two pyramids, joined somehow at their respective peaks, seemed to

[12] Woodrow Wilson, "The Study of Administration," *Political Science Quarterly*, LVI (December, 1941), 494.

settle the question in principle, whatever the practical difficulties.

In addition to its beguiling symmetry, this theory of government seemed to find powerful support in that country to which Americans have always looked for political instruction. One of the first shots in the early battle for civil service reform was Dorman Eaton's book on the civil service in Britain; and later Woodrow Wilson saw in the British system "perfected party government." [13] In Britain, the reformers explained, responsible, disciplined, centralized, programmatic parties compete for public favor. In Parliament the party programs are formed into legislation which is then handed to an efficient, unbiased, politically neutral civil service for execution. The link between the political and the administrative pyramids is provided by the Cabinet and, above all, the Prime Minister: leader of the House of Commons, chief of his political party, and head of the administration.

### 3

While many administrators and students of administration are still content to work quietly in the cloister of the neutral-civil-service idea, others have discovered that the world is not so reasonable or so simple as they were taught in the "reform" school; and, like small boys in similar circumstances, they find a good deal of naughty pleasure in telling everyone about it. In spite of the extension of the merit system and the application of ever more sophisticated principles of administration, there seems to be as much "politics" in federal administration as there ever was. Administration is not, it appears, simply a matter of drawing logical deductions from a general statement of policy. No general statement can be so exhaustive as to permit the civil servant to act on the basis of a series of purely technical calculations, even if he were willing to do so. He is inevitably left with some discretion; he has to exercise his judgment; he has to participate in the making of policy. This is, of course, especially true at the higher levels, but the same principle applies, often in very significant ways, at lower levels as well.

If, then, we need a vast administration staffed largely by permanent officials and if they cannot be confined to merely technical decisions, the result of the attempt to neutralize the

[13] Woodrow Wilson, *Congressional Government* (New York: Meridian Books, 1956), p. 91.

civil service is likely to be not a perfectly efficient and responsive executive machine, but a bureaucratic monster. A civil service free of detailed political control, trained in a purely instrumental science of administration, and insulated from the political life of the community will not be non-political; but it will be politically irresponsible. The spoils system, whatever its other effects, did at least ensure that the bureaucracy shared the political character of the community at large. There is not much serious consideration of going back to the spoils system, but it is argued very strongly that the civil service, being a political institution, must be *representative* of the political community that it serves if it is to be responsible. To the extent that the interests, opinions, and values of civil servants are intimately bound up with those of the community as a whole, any separate "bureaucratic" will or spirit will be out of the question.

Fortunately, in this view, the American civil service does represent the American society with a fair degree of faithfulness. Government offices are not reserved for any favored class or group, and educational prerequisites are usually modest. Appointment depends mainly on an individual's capacity to "do the job," thus permitting representation within the civil service of the diverse political, racial, ethnic, and religious groups which make up the American community. Moreover, entry is not restricted to the bottom rungs of the administrative ladder or to persons just out of school, so there is a constant and healthy infusion of new blood at all levels and a considerable movement between private life and the civil service. The proponents of a "representative bureaucracy" tend to be suspicious of "closed" career systems where there is little or no entry except at the bottom level and where the members ordinarily expect to spend their whole professional lives. The military services have, of course, long been open to suspicion on these grounds. Another favorite object of attack has been the foreign service, where long periods of residence outside the United States, the filling of higher positions exclusively from within the service, and a highly developed esprit de corps are seen to carry a threat of a rigid "inbred" bureaucracy, indifferent or hostile to American democratic values.

It seems, then, that the civil service reform movement has been turned on its head. The early reformers sought, as we have

seen, to take the civil service out of politics and politics out of
the civil service. A neutral civil service, properly organized and
trained, was supposed to serve one party or to implement one
policy just as willingly as any other. More than that, such a
civil service could in principle be transplanted from one political environment to a totally different one, because there was
thought to be, as Woodrow Wilson said, "but one rule of good
administration for all governments alike."[14] In recent years the
idea of a neutral civil service has lost ground. It is now widely
recognized that politics and administration are not capable of
such a strict separation and that, in fact, all interesting administrative questions are political questions. It is seen to be futile
and dangerous to attempt to deprive the civil service of a political function and a political character. The problem, rather, is
to see that the civil service has a political character that will
cause it to perform its political function well. That has been
thought to require in the United States a thoroughly democratic
or representative civil service. What began as a movement to
neutralize the civil service has become a movement to democ-
ratize it.

4

Different as this view of a thoroughly democratized civil service
is from the older one of a thoroughly neutralized civil service,
they have one fundamental feature in common. Both assume
that the civil service is an agency which ought to be responsive
to the will or "values" of the people; both deny that the civil
service should exercise a political will of its own. Only by
questioning this common assumption is it possible to grasp the
fundamental significance of the political role of the modern civil
service. In the remainder of this paper we must consider the
modern civil service not simply as an instrument of elected officials or as a reflector of widespread values, but as a political
agency in its own right, endowed with certain qualities which
give it a reasonable and legitimate claim to share in rule.[15] We
may begin with the 1955 Hoover Commission's proposal to

[14] *Political Science Quarterly*, LVI (December, 1941), 502.
[15] For a comparative and typological study along these lines, see Fritz
Morstein Marx, *The Administrative State* (Chicago: University of Chicago
Press, 1957).

establish in the federal government a "senior civil service."[16]

Although the Hoover Commission made a wide range of suggestions for improvement, it would have left the bulk of the federal service substantially unchanged in character. The civil service would have remained heavily specialized, open to entry at all levels, and as thoroughly "representative" of American life as before. But at the very top level, the Commission proposed to form the best civil servants into an elite corps. The Commission warned against a blanket inclusion of all top civil servants into the new cadre, for this would defeat the purpose of establishing a small, necessarily exclusive, corps of public servants of the very highest quality. These senior civil servants would be expected to exercise a strict political neutrality; they would refrain from defending controversial policies before Congress and from making other public statements which might taint them with partisanship and thus undermine their usefulness as civil servants. Indeed, the Commission was criticized for trying to revive the old idea of a perfectly neutral civil service along British lines. It is true that the Hoover Commission, like the old civil service reformers, drew heavily (though in this case silently) on British experience; but the evidence suggests that its understanding of how British government works was considerably better.

The British civil service was not, is not, and could not be "neutral" in the sense in which the early reformers understood that term: a well-tuned machine responding automatically to whatever political instructions are fed into it. The official conduct of the British civil servant is certainly characterized by a scrupulous neutrality as between political parties. Even his private opinions are unlikely to be strongly partisan, though there are less severe formal restrictions on his political activities than on those of his American counterpart. But, far from resting on a purely technical concern with administration, this nonpartisanship rests on the agreement between the civil service and the political parties on political fundamentals. The civil servant knows that he can serve faithfully even a party with which he has serious disagreement, because in these party matters reason-

---

[16] Commission on Organization of the Executive Branch of the Government, *Personnel and Civil Service* and *Task Force Report on Personnel and Civil Service* (Washington: U.S.G.P.O., 1955).

able and honorable Britons may differ. Somewhat remote from the most active sphere of political life, he is likely to acquire a habitual moderation, avoiding extremes and reminding himself that his disagreements with his political superior about the issues of the day are insignificant compared with the deep agreement on which they rest. The British civil servant is "neutral," not because he is above all a civil servant but because he is above all British.

Thus the British civil servant's neutrality or, more precisely, non-partisanship, has a political base. He can stand aloof from disputes between parts of the body politic precisely because he shares so thoroughly in the consensus about the character of the whole. But he also has a positive political role. While he carries out party programs with which he may disagree, he also helps to modify the partisanship of his political superiors. To give but one example, Labour partisans often expressed, prior to 1945, a doubt whether the predominantly middle-class civil service would loyally and effectively carry out the programs of a Labour Government. When the test came, not only did the civil service not sabotage Labour programs, but there was surprisingly little evidence of bureaucratic dragging of feet. According to Labour's Prime Minister, "There were certainly some people in the Labour Party who doubted whether the civil servants would give fair play to a socialist government, but all doubts disappeared with experience."[17] It is true that the responsiveness of the civil service to Labour programs was helped by the changed social and political composition of the service, though there was least change in the crucial top ranks. But it is also true that the Labour Government proved to be much less of a threat to the fundamental political consensus than many, including many Labourites, had expected. Quite a different situation would have existed had Labour really tried to engineer a socialist revolution and had it cast aside the traditional institutions and conventions that contain British political life—and a different civil service would have been required. As it was, the old civil service dog certainly learned and loyally performed some new Labour tricks, but the Labour Ministers also learned something from the

[17] The Right Hon. The Earl Attlee, "Civil Servants, Ministers, Parliament and the Public," in William A. Robson (ed.), *The Civil Service in Britain and France* (London: The Hogarth Press, 1956), p. 16.

civil service. As one of those Ministers, Herbert Morrison, described it:

> The relationship between the Minister and the civil servants should be—and usually is—that of colleagues working together in a team, co-operative partners seeking to advance the public interest and the efficiency of the Department. . . . The partnership should be alive and virile, rival ideas and opinions should be fairly considered, and the relationship of all should be one of mutual respect—on the understanding, of course, that the Minister's decision is final and must be loyally and helpfully carried out, and that he requires efficient and energetic service.[18]

But does this kind of partnership have any meaningful or legitimate application in the United States? Obviously there are difficulties standing in the way of a transfer of British institutions to American shores. Thus for example, although the call of the Hoover Commission for strict "political neutrality" by the senior civil service did not (contrary to the views of some critics) imply acceptance of the old idea of a merely technical civil service, it was open to the criticism that it took too little account of the complex internal articulation of the American political system. Granting the validity of this criticism does not, however, necessarily mean that the notion of a partnership between political party leaders and civil servants is inapplicable in the United States, although it does point to the different and more complex form that an American partnership must take.

This question of the kind of political neutrality that can be expected or desired of American civil servants is closely connected with a feature of the American Constitution that has long embarrassed party and civil service reformers, namely the system of checks and balances. The reformers, firmly persuaded by the logic of the two pyramids (that elaboration of a misunderstanding of British government), tended to regard the separation of powers as a "defect" in the American system, to be remedied either by drastic constitutional change or through the informal agency of reformed parties in control of a reformed administration. Even in their most generous and patriotic mood, they could scarcely see in this central feature of the American

[18] *Government and Parliament* (London: Oxford University Press, 1954), pp. 318-19.

Constitution anything but a curiosity of the eighteenth-century mind—a once harmless nuisance grown under modern conditions into an intolerable obstacle to responsible and efficient government. The very fact that the civil service is constitutionally not simply subordinate to either the President or the Congress tends to obscure lines of command and, incidentally, to increase the political influence of the civil service. It is easy to see why the reformers, with their idea of a neutral civil service, thought that such a system could produce nothing but confusion and irresponsibility.

If, however, the civil service is regarded not as a neutral instrument but as a political institution, then the constitutional system of checks and balances appears in a different light. While the framers of the Constitution doubtless failed to anticipate the full significance of the administrative state, there is nevertheless a close harmony between the original intention of the system of checks and balances and the political role of the modern civil service. Without entering fully into this subject, we may say that the system of checks and balances was an attempt to institutionalize moderation; and one of the important ways it does this in modern American government is by adding to the political weight of the civil service which, more than any of the other active agencies of government, stands for moderation. Of course the Founders recognized that their "inventions of prudence" were not a sufficient condition of good government and might sometimes prove a positive handicap, and we must recognize the same about a politically influential civil service. But if the civil service is a political institution with a political function, it does not appear unreasonable that it should have some political power. In what follows we shall consider what the bureaucracy, in partnership with political parties, can and does contribute to American government.[19]

5

One manifestation of the basic problem of government by political parties is the fact that politicians who run for office in their capacity as leaders of organized parts, or parties, of the

[19] Of what follows it may be said, with Blackstone, "This is the spirit of our constitution: not that I assert it is in fact quite so perfect as I have here endeavoured to describe it. . . ." I *Commentaries* 172.

body politic are expected to assume a responsibility for the government of the whole. This formulation is obviously incomplete. American political parties themselves undertake to form particular individuals, groups, interests, and opinions into some kind of whole. This is not the place to discuss this broad responsibility or the various means by which American parties discharge it. It may be observed, however, that one means is the appointment of men who are not distinctively party men to fill even high political positions, to say nothing of the appointment of members of the opposite party. Rexford Tugwell was not a Democrat in the same sense as James Farley; Charles Wilson was not a Republican in the same sense as Arthur Summerfield. And Harvard professors, it may be assumed, are not Democrats in the same sense as persons whose whole career is associated with that party. Yet in spite of this and other qualifications, the fact remains that in a very important sense our system of government gives to a part the responsibility for governing the whole.

It is notorious that party politicians tend to learn moderation and responsibility when in office; but it is perhaps less generally recognized that one of their main teachers is the civil service. The common contrast between the politician, as the "practical man" experienced in "real life" and in touch with the wants and needs of the people, and the bureaucrat, as the remote, paper-shuffling office boy, is grossly overdrawn. In the first place, many civil servants have, in their particular fields, a kind of direct contact with the people and experience of the problems of government which even the politician whose ear never leaves the ground cannot possibly match. Moreover, modern government is to a large extent conducted by "shuffling papers," and it is of vital importance that they be shuffled well. Finally, a large part of the proposals for new policies and legislation come up through the civil service. Not only do civil servants exercise discretion in interpreting and applying the commands of their political superiors; they participate intimately in the formulation of those commands. They make proposals of their own and fight for them; they comment on the proposals of their political superiors—and may fight against them. They make a vital contribution to the process of deciding what is to be done. Government would come to a standstill if our "closet statesmen" in the civil service suddenly started doing only what they were told.

In the United States, of course, due partly to the constitutional system of checks and balances, the civil servant does not and perhaps cannot be expected to confine his statesmanship to the closet. Indeed, one of the peculiarities of American public administration is the fact that the civil servant may have more political knowledge and skill, even in the rather narrow sense, than his "political" superior. And he is almost certain to have, at least at first, more familiarity with the politics involved in actually running the government. A new Secretary or Assistant Secretary will normally find himself heavily dependent upon his experienced civil servants to facilitate not only the internal management of the agency but also its relations with Congress, interested organizations, other agencies of government, and even the White House itself. Compared with his counterpart in England, the American political executive has, generally speaking, to steer through political waters that are more cloudy and turbulent and to do it with less training and experience. Little wonder that he has to place extensive trust in the political judgment of experienced pilots in the civil service.

It is true that much of the contribution of the civil service to the art of government, even in the United States, is of a restraining and even negative kind. The civil servant, especially at the higher levels, has seen many programs tried, and many failures; even the successful innovations have usually fallen short of their makers' hopes. His experience has caused him to be sensitive to difficulties; he is an expert in seeking out unanticipated consequences. Even after a new policy has been decided upon, the civil servant is likely to explain, perhaps at exasperating length, why it cannot possibly be carried out the way his political chief wants. The civil servant is full of procedures, rules, and regulations, and he will (if he is performing properly) instruct his chief in the reasons for them. Orderly administration is not the most important quality of good government and it may sometimes have to be sacrificed to higher ends, but it is, generally speaking, indispensable. The cautious prudence and orderliness which tend to characterize the civil service are precisely that part of practical wisdom in which the party politician is likely to be deficient. The political leader in the United States is at least as much in need of the "prudent counsel and efficient aid" of "able and judicious men" as was the English statesman of the nineteenth century addressed by Sir Henry Taylor;[20] and he will find many of them in the civil service.

The special kind of practical wisdom that characterizes the civil servant points to a more fundamental political function of the bureaucracy, namely to bring to bear on public policy its distinctive view of the common good or its way of looking at questions about the common good. The preoccupation of the civil service with rules and regulations, for example, is not aimed merely at orderly administration, important as that is. The rules and regulations, and the principle that there should *be* rules and regulations, represent a certain principle of justice, if only the principle of treating equals equally. Similar considerations apply to the civil servant's predilection for the way things have been done in the past. Generally speaking, to follow precedents is orderly, reasonable, and fair. One of the basic principles of American government is that governmental action should ordinarily be taken on the basis of established rules, however irritating that may sometimes be to a politician with a substantive program to put through. Like judges, civil servants have a special responsibility to preserve the rule of law.

Civil servants also bear a similarity to judges in their possession of what is, for most practical purposes, permanent tenure in office. Of course, like judges, they are influenced by the election returns—and it would be dangerous if they were not; but they have a degree of insulation from shifting political breezes. The rhythm of their official lives and thoughts is not governed so strictly as is that of the political executive by periodic elections. Their position enables them to mitigate the partisanship of party politics, and it gives them some protection from the powerful temptation, to which the party politician is always subject, to serve the people's inclinations rather than their interests.

Clement Attlee described the higher civil servant in Britain as having, in addition to long personal experience, "that mysterious tradition of the office wherein is somehow embalmed the wisdom of past generations."[21] The civil service in the United States is of course far less time-encrusted, but here too the higher civil servant will ordinarily have long experience in government, nearly always longer than his political chiefs. More-

[20] *The Statesman* (New York: Mentor Books, 1958), p. 108.
[21] In Robson (ed.), *The Civil Service in Britain and France*, p. 17.

154

over the duties of the civil servant and the way he works—his concern for written records, for example—tend to make him conscious of the "long-termness" of political decisions to a degree that is unusual for transient party politicians. At its best, the civil service is a kind of democratic approximation to an hereditary aristocracy whose members are conscious of representing an institution of government which extends into the past and into the future beyond the life of any individual member. In our mobile democracy, the civil service is one of the few institutions we have for bringing the accumulated wisdom of the past to bear upon political decisions.

Perhaps the most important political contribution that a civil service can make is, of all those we have considered, the one the American civil service makes least. Neither the bureaucracy nor political parties merely "represents" or reflects the American polity; they also help to shape and guide that polity, and they perform this function by what they are as well as by what they do. The character of a country's public servants is one of the determinants of the character of its people. When George Washington sought honest, honorable, and loyal gentlemen to fill the public offices of the new country, he was concerned not only with getting the work of government done but also with distributing the patronage of government in such a way as to set the public stamp of approval on certain human qualities. When Andrew Jackson established the system of rotation in public office, he had the same broad objective in mind, but he sought to elevate the common man in the place of the gentleman. And what the civil service reformers feared most about the spoils system was the effect on the political character of the people of the example set by the kind of men which the spoils system tended to elevate. "Politics cannot be made a mere trade," George Curtis argued, "without dangerously relaxing the moral character of the country."[22] In the words of Dorman Eaton,

> It is in the struggles for office, and the opportunities for gain in the exercise of official power, that selfishness, deception, and partisan zeal have their everlasting contest with virtue, patriotism, and duty. It is in that contest that statesmen and demagogues, patriots and intriguers, the good citizen and the venal office seeker, all

[22] The Reform of the Civil Service," in *Orations and Addresses*, II, 43.

the high and all the low influences of political life, meet face to face, and by the balance of power, for good or for evil, give character to politics and determine the morality of nations.[23]

Except for the removal of corruption, however, the reformers gave little thought to the kind of character and morality which their neutral, merely technical civil service would exemplify. One indication of the result is the fact that American civil servants themselves, though they may be thoroughly devoted to serving the common good, ordinarily prefer to identify themselves by their profession or occupation or "job" rather than by their public service. It is thought more respectable to be an agricultural economist or a personnel specialist than to be a civil servant. Not the least of the merits of the Hoover Commission proposal for a senior civil service is the influence such a corps of public servants might have on American life and character by restoring to a place of honor and respect the title of "civil servant."

The civil service is, then, in possession of certain institutional qualities which give it a title to share with elected officials in rule. It has a distinctive competence in the art of government and a unique knowledge of the problems of government, without which stable and intelligent government under modern conditions would be literally impossible. It has, moreover, a distinctive view of the common good which can guide and supplement the view likely to be taken by elected party politicians. On the foundation of its procedures, its rules, its institutional memory and foresight, its traditions, its skepticism of political panaceas, and its protection from the whims of popularity, the civil service stands for the continuity and wholeness of American government.

### 6

It is not to be denied that bureaucracy suffers characteristic limitations and defects. Neither the party politician nor the bureaucrat has an unqualified claim to rule; neither is unqualifiedly competent or entitled to act on behalf of the whole people. Under ordinary circumstances the actual conduct of American government is in the charge of a partnership between them. We have emphasized the contributions of the bureaucratic part of

[23] *Civil Service in Great Britain*, pp. 423–24.

this partnership, because they are less generally understood. But as the civil servant teaches, so also he is taught by the party politician. The civil servant is likely, for example, to overdo his concern with procedures and rules. He may be blind to the fact that procedural justice can do substantive injustice. It may be necessary for his political chief to show him that procedures have become so complex as to defeat their purpose or that the original reason for a rule has disappeared. While the civil servant may take a longer view of the common good, his view may also be distorted by a preoccupation with one program or a rather narrow range of programs. The broader range of responsibilities of the political chief may provide a corrective.[24] Moreover, although the civil servant bears the immediate responsibility for government because he does (or is closer to) the actual governing, he does not bear the final responsibility. He may instruct his political chief, he may advise him, guide him, even manage him— but he does not have the last word. This means that he may be overruled, for good reasons or bad; but it also means that his way of thinking and acting is molded in part by the fact of his formal subordination. Even at his best he is not a political captain but a faithful, wise, and influential counsellor and servant.[25]

[24] As one civil service bureau chief explained, "The assistant secretary and I deal with the same people and do many of the same sorts of things, but the task of the assistant secretary is to keep me from losing touch with the mass of the people, from becoming too ingrown. The political executive provides that sensitivity to the public pulse. He and I approach our similar jobs from different angles. If we can learn to talk each other's language, we make a good team." Marver H. Bernstein, *The Job of the Federal Executive* (Washington: The Brookings Institution, 1958), p. 49.

[25] "I remember that I went to my new secretary and said: 'I think a man coming into your job should have his own men around him. I am a career employee, but if you should decide to have your own man in this job, I hope you will first give me a trial because I think I can help you. But if you decide to have your own man, there will be no difficulty about it. All you need to do is tell me. If you want to try me first, I will attempt to give you all the facts bearing on your particular problem, and I will give them to you as accurately and impartially as I can. You will have to have faith in me until you learn to know me better. If you want me to make a recommendation, I will do so. If we get to the point where I cannot live with your decisions, I will get out. I will fight you outside the government, but I won't do so in the government. I won't make any end runs on you. Now, you don't know me from Adam, and you never heard of me before in all likelihood. You don't know whether I am going to live up to that statement or not. You will have to take it on faith.' The secretary really needed me, but he didn't know it yet. As it turned out, we got along very well." *Ibid.*, p. 191.

This is connected with a final limitation of bureaucracy. Although a good civil service is one of the guardians of the traditional political wisdom of a regime, "sometimes it is necessary," as Attlee says, "to react violently against the tradition which was formed for a different state of society."[26] While it is difficult to imagine Lord Attlee reacting violently against anything, it is clear that traditional bureaucratic wisdom may not suit changed circumstances. The very tradition which it is the responsibility of the bureaucrat to carry forward may require fundamental redefinition, and that is a task for which his duties, training, and experience disqualify him. During such times of crisis, "administration" does become radically subordinate to "politics"; the institution of the civil service does become to a much greater extent than usual an instrument of the man who is President. The peak of the spoils system is generally regarded as having come during Lincoln's first administration, and Lincoln removed the incumbents of almost all offices under his immediate control. He used the spoils of office to help bind together the Republican Party, the North, and thereby the Union. So much was this the paramount aim that, according to one historian, Lincoln "made no attempt to obtain the men best fitted to perform the functions of the various offices, except in case of the very highest; for minor places he did not even insist that a man be fit."[27] The Civil War is an extreme example, but it is not the only one. The transformation which the civil service underwent at the hands of Franklin Roosevelt is well known. Roosevelt gave a new meaning to the civil service and to the Democratic Party in the course of giving a new meaning to American political life as a whole. During such critical times, the question of bureaucracy as such is almost entirely subordinated to the more fundamental question of political reconstruction. It is not unfair to say of the bureaucracy (and perhaps of political parties too) that it contributes least to government in the most important cases, provided it is remembered that a government requires a capacity for everyday competence, prudence, and public-spiritedness, as well as a capacity for greatness.

[26] In Robson (ed.), *The Civil Service in Britain and France*, p. 17.
[27] Carl Russell Fish, *The Civil Service and the Patronage* (Cambridge: Harvard University Press, 1920), p. 170.